Lalita Iyer is a Mumbai-based journalist, columnist and author of *The Whole Shebang: Sticky Bits of Being a Woman* and *I'm Pregnant, Not Terminally Ill, You Idiot!* She has also written for children (*The Boy Who Swallowed a Nail and Other Stories*) and edited two anthologies (*Grandma Tales* and *Grandpa Tales*). She was earlier managing editor at *Filmfare* and deputy editor at *HT Cafe*. She has written extensively on pop culture, feminism, travel, food, parenting, Bollywood and relationships.

On Sridevi

'She was big in the little things she did with her performances, which made them memorable. When you watched her in *Khuda Gawah,* she was not a Bachchan heroine showing up for the mandatory two songs. She was an equal, a powerhouse, because she could balance the aura of a star with being such a fine actor.'—Anupama Chopra

'Imagine having the opportunity to flirt and interact with the camera from the age of four—it's a unique opportunity any actor can get, and it can only add richness and texture to one's craft. It's like growing up with a gold mine inside; Sridevi didn't have to go out looking for it.'—Adil Hussain

'She had fantastic range. The way she dominated the industry in the '80s, she totally owned it. She made a unique connection with her audience. They came only to see her.'—Poonam Saxena

'Sridevi was such a bright, happy spark who lit up the screen. She had this unusual quality of always leaving a little bit of her in you, whether it was her bangles in *Chandni* or her blue sari in *Mr India* or even her stubborn pigtail in *Sadma*. You always wanted to watch those movies over and over because, in a sense, they never left you.'—Maria Goretti

SRIDEVI

Queen of Hearts

Lalita Iyer

First published by Westland Publications Private Limited in 2018
61, 2nd Floor, Silverline Building, Alapakkam Main Road, Maduravoyal, Chennai 600095

Westland and the Westland logo are the trademarks of Westland Publications Private Limited, or its affiliates.

ISBN: 9789387578593

10 9 8 7 6 5 4 3 2 1

Typeset in Arno Pro by SÜRYA, New Delhi
Printed at Thomson Press (India) Ltd.

For Amma

CONTENTS

Foreword

I REMEMBER WATCHING *Sadma* in 1983. I came out of the cinema hall, utterly depressed. My throat was dry. I went home and did not feel like eating or talking to anybody for two days.

I could not have imagined before that a film could have this impact on a person. I was only twenty. At the time, I could not have conceived that I would work with Sridevi one day.

What struck me the most about Sridevi were her eyes, which were the gateways to her soul. They never betrayed a shred of emotion outside the sets. They were almost transparent, yet filled with artistry, which transformed raw emotions into a highly skilled and potent dose of 'humanness' for the audience. I was mesmerised.

When I met her, the first words I uttered to her were, 'I didn't eat for two days after watching *Sadma*.' She looked at me and instantly her eyes filled up. I am sure she fathomed the honestly and sincerity in my confession. She smiled shyly and said, 'Thank you', and we started our rehearsals for *English Vinglish*.

In the hours, days, weeks and months that I spent in her company, I gathered that she was one of the most quiet, sensitive and vulnerable actors I have ever met, who had worked hard to elevate herself to the level of a fine artist. She understood, I believe, how to communicate with the Indian audience in an Indian way. In our ancient, traditional theatrical performances, especially in Kudiyattam and Kathakali, the actors, even when they are speaking to each other, always face the audience. They perform for the audience with utmost respect and with the intent of uplifting the spectators to a greater reality. That is the fundamental purpose of any traditional Indian performance—to lift the audience from the micro to the macro. However, most modern Indian actors, whether trained in drama schools or not, are influenced by the Western school of acting, which believes there is a fourth wall between the audience and the performer—allowing the audience to peep into actors' lives secretly. Therefore, they are, to some extent, untrue in believing that the audience does not exist. If not untrue, it is definitely a half-truth.

Sridevi, on the other hand, maybe because of her exposure to Indian classical dance, or for reasons unknown to me, always seemed to have a sacred relationship with the audience, and therefore she performed for them. Not to show off, but to bare her soul, retaining the intense truthfulness of the situations in the script and her responses to the various characters, in the moment. She was one of a kind, almost unique in possessing this skill. Despite acting *for* the camera, she never was false.

On the other hand, a lot of Indian actors act for the camera, but without the truthfulness of the situation or the moment; thus their acting does not impact us deep inside. Much has been said about Sridevi's comic timing. In my experience, comic timing is purely about timing. The context could be light or grave. Perfect timing in responding to a situation or a co-actor is a consequence of one's intense awareness and attentiveness to the moment. I feel that Sridevi's practice of quietude (many people have talked about how quiet she used to be on film sets) was the reason for her perfect timing. By keeping quiet on the sets, she, I believe, contained her energies from being dissipated.

Quietude also leads to deep sensitivity and was responsible for the grace she possessed. In modern actors, I am increasingly seeing a lack of grace, dignity or sensitivity of the intensity that Sridevi possessed. She was a unique actor with a uniquely Indian style of acting. I wish she was still alive. I wish she could have passed on her mastery to others. I wish *English Vinglish* 2 could be made.

Adil Hussain
July 2018

Note from the Author

I DID NOT know Sridevi. I am quite sure she did not know me.

I wasn't invited to her fiftieth birthday party, nor was I part of her karva chauth group or PTA. I didn't meet her at the gym or the spa, nor did I share a nutritionist with her. I didn't follow her on social media, neither did I change my DP to 'Hawa Hawai' when she died.

I didn't even have her phone number.

During my journalistic career, roughly from 2005-14, Sridevi was mostly out of circulation, taking her motherhood sabbatical. Except for that window when *English Vinglish* was released and she was briefly available for interviews. I worked at *Filmfare* then and the whole world was jockeying to interview her, enticing the PR mafia, which now controlled who spoke to whom and when. You couldn't talk to movie people like you used to, even until a few years ago. It was all too much for me.

I chose to interview Adil Hussain instead.

So my one window of interviewing Sridevi was gone.

In any case, I always knew she wasn't an interviewer's delight, so I was happy that she continued to live in my head as she did—full of mischief, vulnerability and possibility.

While I was growing up, movie stars were the 'other'—their

lives, their real stories were always beyond our reach. You couldn't be throwing emojis at them, commenting on their Instagram posts, tweeting to them, posting on their timelines. And maybe it was better that way, because the few times that I did meet my idols years later as a journalist, or saw them up close, the bubble burst very swiftly.

Growing up, I had an uncle who worked as a proofreader with *The Times of India*; he hoarded his complimentary copies of *Filmfare* like they were gold. Visitors could have access to them if they asked nicely, but you had to read and return them. They could not be borrowed or taken out of the house.

Filmfare, even then, didn't do much gossip; there were other magazines for that sort of stuff. I caught sporadic glimpses of *Frankly Speaking by Devi* in *Star & Style* (she made me want to be a film gossip columnist), or *Neeta's Natter* in *Stardust* in the homes of other relatives. Whenever I was ill, my father got me a copy of *Stardust* and I felt immensely better walking into a world that was so near and yet so far.

I don't remember reading about Sridevi in any of these, because she was never a part of my childhood. I watched my first Sridevi film when school was already behind me, and the pressures and rigours of college life and youth had begun.

Soon after Sridevi's death, when Westland asked me if I could write a book about her, I found myself saying yes, instinctively, in the manner of: 'I really like her, so maybe I can wing that.'

No, it wasn't overconfidence. I just wanted to be the one picked for the job.

I went straight home and watched *ChaalBaaz* from start to finish, hoping, praying that Sridevi would still have the same effect on me as she did when I'd first watched it. She did. But now she was gone. Forever.

That was when the intensity of the tragedy struck me. I just sat and watched more of her films for the rest of the night.

Before I even heard a formal confirmation from the publisher, I was neck deep in Sridevi movies. This time I also wanted to watch all the Tamil films I had missed before she came to Bollywood. My mother looked both amused and pleased and was eager to be the translator of words and phrases I couldn't understand.

How often in your life do you get to kill yourself like this? To spend days, weeks, watching films of your favourite screen icon, pausing, rewinding, laughing, crying, making notes, asking your mother to join in with you, discovering her favourite Sridevi movies—rinse, repeat. To notice the tiny details, delicate nuances that you had missed the first time you watched them, when all you were looking for was entertainment.

How often do you go to sleep thinking of dialogues, dance, scenes—the times Sridevi made you laugh and the times she made you cry and the times she somehow made you feel you-er than you. How often do you wake up thinking of lines to finish a chapter or start a new one? How often do you find yourself staring at the mirror and going, '*Awi wiwi wiwi wiwi*', making a Sridevi-face, trying a trick-stumble?

Yes, I enjoyed how she filled my life intensely in those months and occupied a considerable part of my conscious and subconscious mind. It gave me immense joy and a few sleepless nights, but it made me go inside of me in a way that I hadn't in a while.

The question then was: what does one call this book? Is this her biography? I don't think so. Will this be of historic or academic interest? I don't know. Does it have juicy interviews, salacious stuff? I am afraid not. Did I have access to her inner circle? I didn't see the point.

In the beginning I did chase the usual suspects, and except one or two who wrote or texted back immediately or picked up the phone, the rest dodged and stalled, and I couldn't be bothered with their PR mafia.

I told myself I was writing a fan's tribute and about what I thought mattered. Sridevi made me believe that things don't always have to add up—that you could be badass, yet vulnerable; playful, yet responsible; sexy, yet klutzy; quiet, yet be able to summon the super strength of a goddess. That there is no *one* way to be a woman. And that laughing at yourself is a talent. She taught me that you don't always have to fit in; if you truly believe in the things you do, you will still stand out. Body-shamed for her 'thunder thighs', often ridiculed for being dubbed in many of her films, Sridevi may not always have had a smooth ride. However, there was a quiet defiance in the way she took on every role that was offered to her and made the most of it.

For those who were not Sridevi fans, she was always too much. Her nose was too big, her voice was too girly, her pitch was too high, her face was too babyish, her eyes were too large, her lips were too wobbly, her hips were too wide.

For the rest of us, she was just right.

1

How I Met My Mother

MY MOTHER AND I don't agree on most things.

We agree on Sridevi.

It was just after my Std X board exams in 1983 when I convinced Amma to take me to watch *Sadma.* I had missed *Himmatwala* as it had released during my board exams but had heard about this new heroine Sridevi and wanted to see her on screen. (*Solva Sawan* came and went a long time ago without a whimper and since it was an adult movie, it was totally out of the question.)

Her backstory, I had no clue about, except that she was from the south. It was ironic that as a TamBram growing up in Bombay (it was still Bombay then), I had no sense of connectedness to my roots.

I was a fan of Kamal Haasan though, having watched him in *Ek Duje ke Liye* and *Sanam Teri Kasam.* I was quite taken in by his dancing and acting skills, even though Appa wondered why he had to enter the Hindi film industry when people were so crazy about him down south.

Growing up in the 1970s on a healthy diet of once-a-month haircut-and-movie outings with Appa that featured Amitabh

Bachchan, Shashi Kapoor, Shatrughan Sinha, Rishi Kapoor, Rekha, Rakhee, Hema Malini, Jaya Bhaduri, Sanjeev Kumar, Zeenat Aman and Parveen Babi, movies were my everything. There was no television and no internet and no toys. Only a radio, which was my only companion. We never got *filmi* magazines at home, and no one went to beauty parlours to read them.

My occasional source of movie gossip were my relatives and their stash of magazines. When I came home after reading a *Filmfare* or a *Stardust* cover to cover during the summer or Diwali holidays (the time when one went relative-hopping), I had enough stories to tell my classmates for at least a month. But, in those days, one did not really miss access to the private lives of film stars. One just adored them for what they were on screen.

Amma and I never had a cinema thing going. All my movie experiences from childhood were matinees with Appa, who was the real movie buff. Besides, Amma had written off Hindi cinema for a while (the last one she had liked was *Khubsoorat*, 1980). They lacked a certain gravitas she was used to in Tamil cinema. She believed they were too showy, not realistic enough, the acting was not up to par, they didn't know how to tell a story. She had been raised on a staple diet of south Indian cinema (Tamil, Kannada and Malayalam) that I didn't know much about, and didn't consider 'cool enough' at that age. Plus there was not much access unless we visited my aunt in Matunga; she lived close to Aurora Cinema, the haven of Tamil films.

Besides, Amma couldn't relate to the women. Zeenat Aman was too sexy, Rekha was not loyal to her south Indian genes and spoke Hindi like a north Indian, Hema Malini never grew up from '*Nahinnnnn*' and was annoying with her predictable beauty, Parveen Babi was too Anglo, Rakhee sobbed too much, Neetu Singh wore tiny dresses, and so on.

But *Sadma* changed that. For a bit.

Sadma was labelled 'Adults Only', but I convinced Amma that I was grown up enough now that I had passed out of school. Also, I had listened to the radio trailers: it was about a girl who had lost her memory—how adult could that be? Besides, no one checked IDs in Kalyan, where we then lived. Amma agreed, and I was relieved. I had her at Sridevi though.

Sadma is the story of a young girl who slips into severe retrograde amnesia after an accident and then finds herself in a brothel from which she is rescued by a school teacher, Somu (Kamal Haasan), who brings her to Ooty where he lives and teaches. Nehalata/Reshmi (Sridevi) is, in effect, a twenty-five-year-old body living in a six-year-old's mind. As she gingerly steps off the charming steam-engine train at Ooty, she is both intrigued and delighted by the things she sees around her. She tries to lick the water dripping off the rooftop of the train, and squirms at its metallic taste. With her resolute pigtail, which refuses to stay straight and always twists upwards, she quickly steps off, trying to keep pace with Somu, and on the way gets distracted by a green flag sticking out of the coupling between the rail bogies and tries to reach for it. '*Yeh kiska jhhanda hain?*' (Whose flag is this?) she asks, trying to make a grab for it, just as the guard approaches, which scares her away. None of this seemed incongruous, even as it was enacted by a full-grown, voluptuous woman. Cherubic, vulnerable, playful, with a complete lack of guile, Sridevi fit the part beautifully.

Acting like a child is one thing. Being a child is quite another. Sridevi had 'become' the six-year-old. There are many other scenes in the movie that are etched in my memory, but then this book is more than just about *Sadma.*

In the hospital scene post the accident, Sridevi (now in amnesia) comes face to face with her father (Arvind Deshpande) and fails to recognise him. Twitching her nose and her lower lip, her face instantly transforms into that of a child. It was mind-boggling. '*Mere* Daddy *ke bahut baal hai. Tumhare toh baal hi nahi hai*' (My father has a lot of hair on his head; you have no hair), she says, in between sobs. This made Amma laugh; she whispered to me in the dark that as a child I had said something similar to a cousin whose father was the only bald man in a family of hirsute abundance.

Sadma, 1983

By the interval, both Amma and I were in a warm, fuzzy place; she was already welling up at the bond that had developed between the rescued and the rescuer. He can't escape her womanhood, but he is protective about the child in her. Beaming at me for having brought her to a Hindi movie she liked, she said, 'This is *Moondram Pirai,* and it's almost as good.'

That was big.

Amma's condescension towards Hindi films was slightly redeemed. As we both came away sobbing from the cinema hall, she said, 'You should see her Tamil movies. You will know. This is nothing.'

It was a turning point for me. So far I had not exhibited any affinity towards my south Indian roots (except for learning Bharatanatyam). I had driven my Carnatic music teacher away. I could speak laughable Tamil but very good Hindi and Marathi, and I had never watched any Tamil movies. I knew that once a month, they did show them on Doordarshan, which has never been known for its curation.

We had recently acquired a Keltron television, although a large amount of time was spent beating it up to get good reception. It usually had to be kept switched on for at least half an hour before the stipulated programme for it to settle into some kind of non-blurry state.

The next time we were in Matunga, we had a VCR bonanza. Four Sridevi movies were rented and we watched them back-to-back. *Moondram Pirai, Meendum Kokila, Sigappu Rojakkal, Varumayin Niram Sivappu*—all Kamal-Sridevi films in Tamil. I remember one particular scene in *Meendum Kokila* in which we all laughed till our tummies hurt: Kokila (Sridevi) accompanies her husband Mani (Kamal Haasan) to a formal dinner at his boss's place, where the socially inept Kokila makes an attempt to eat *baadusha* (a sweet) with a spoon and a fork, sending it flying onto a colleague's bosom. When Mani reprimands her for this, she replies, 'Who would have thought their baadushas would be so hard?' In *Varumayin Niram Sivappu,* Amma and her sisters hummed along as Kamal Haasan added his words to Sridevi's tunes in the famous song '*Sippi irukkudu*', set in the hills of Himachal Pradesh.

Perhaps that's why Amma was pleased that with the entry of Sridevi, she would have some real films to watch in Hindi. Sridevi was pure and innocent and funny and childlike and angry and sad with equal intensity. Anyone who could make you laugh and cry in equal measure got Amma's vote. That is why Kamal Haasan was her favourite too.

Her joy was short-lived however. Soon after came *Maqsad, Mawaali, Justice Chaudhury, Tohfa, Masterji* and the lot, each one more ridiculous than the next. A disappointed Amma decided that Sridevi did the wrong thing by joining 'Hindi filims', because now she no longer did the Tamil cinema that Amma was so proud of. She blamed Sridevi's dilution as an actor on the 'Hindi cinema' effect, where everything is 'show-sha' and nothing is of real substance.

I reminded her of Vyjayanthimala, Hema Malini and Rekha—also south Indians, who had made it big in Hindi cinema. 'Yes, but how many hit south Indian films had they done before joining Bollywood?' Amma asked. She had a point.

To Amma, Sridevi was 'us' and the rest were 'them'.

Meanwhile, Sri was laughing all the way to the bank and

being called the female Amitabh Bachchan. I couldn't help noticing that even in the trashiest of films, she lived the role like she believed in it—no matter how many leather skirts with leotards and boots or wigs she wore or how many whips she cracked or lenses she changed.

But, once in a while, there was a gem like a *Mr India* or a *Chandni* (which we both loved), or a *ChaalBaaz* (which is my favourite Sridevi movie), or a *Lamhe,* which surprisingly Amma appreciated, though it was too radical for the masses. (I remember that years ago, she had actually been okay with Sridevi in the role of Rajinikanth's stepmother in *Moondru Mudichu.*)

As youth, career and other pursuits engaged me, Amma and I drifted apart, and there was no Sridevi to hold us together. I left home and had neither the time nor the inclination to watch her films anymore. After a few years, she went virtually underground post marriage and motherhood; and we got busy with our lives.

Years later, when I became a mother, Amma and I had a *Sadma*-like moment again while watching *English Vinglish.* 'This I like,' she said, turning to me during the interval.

Sridevi was back in our lives, although she had never left our hearts.

'When you do something all your life, you never forget it,' Amma said, wiping away a tear, as we walked home from the theatre.

'What do you mean?' (Since I had never interviewed Sridevi, research about her past had never crossed my mind.)

'Don't you know she has been acting since the age of four?'

And that's how I met my mother again.

2

Child, Interrupted

Surmayee ankhiyon main
Nanha munna ek sapana de jaa re
Nindiya ke udate paakhi re
Ankhiyon main aaja saathi re
Raa ree raa rum o raaree rum
Raa ree raa rum o raaree rum

(Leave a beautiful little dream
In the kohl-lined eyes
O dear bird with sleep-wings,
Perch on the eyelids and sing…)

—Lyrics from *Sadma,* 1983

SHREE AMMA YANGER AYYAPAN (Sridevi to most of us) was born on 13 August 1963 in Sivakasi, Tamil Nadu, to a Naidu family. Her father, Ayyapan Yanger, was a lawyer who belonged to Sivakasi and her mother, Rajeswari, was from Tirupati, Andhra Pradesh. They had two daughters—the older, Sridevi and the younger, Srilatha. It's reported that both her parents had been previously married and her father had two sons from his first marriage—Sateesh and Anand (this would account for the 'two step-brothers' frequently reported in the press). Her mother Rajeswaramma (Rajeswari) was an aspiring actress and had previously been married to small-time actor, Ranga Rao. They had a daughter named Suryakala. Ranga Rao deserted Rajeswari, and Suryakala was raised by her grandparents. (Suryakala's daughter is the south Indian actress Maheshwari, whom Sridevi referred to as her niece.) Sridevi's parents met in Chennai, where her father had his practice and her mother had moved to in search of work.

Sridevi did speak about her childhood and her sister, Srilatha, in some interviews, like this one in *CineBlitz* (August 1985): 'I was a very shy and lonely child. There were just the two of us. My sister, Latha, and I. Even though my parents were devoted to me, I was lonely. I hated crowds and people. The minute I saw more than three or four people in a room, I'd run and hide behind my mother's *pallav*. I was extremely attached to her. I still am.'[1]

With her bright eyes, curly locks and cherubic appeal, it was no wonder that Sridevi had great screen presence even as a child artiste and was much sought after by directors. She seemed comfortable in varied roles, from child god to spoilt brat to a suffering child, and was able to shift gender—playing a boy and a girl with equal ease. However hard it is to imagine, this shy girl did go on to become one of the highest paid child artistes in the country before she became a star.

Sridevi got her first break in the movies as little Lord Muruga in *Thunaivan* (Help) released in 1968. It seems she was

1. http://www.freepressjournal.in/entertainment/i-was-a-very-shy-and-lonely-child-sridevi/646895

also cast as baby Lord Muruga in another Tamil film, *Kandan Karunai*, which was released in 1967, but was later replaced by Master Sridhar during the shooting of the movie. (There is still a blink-and-you-miss-it appearance by Sri in a frame that the director forgot to edit out.)

Thunaivan, 1969

Chinappa Thevar, the producer of *Thunaivan*, initially asked Sridevi's mother to shave off her daughter's curly locks to suit the role. She refused, almost whisking Sridevi off the sets. Finally, a compromise was reached and she played Baby Muruga with shoulder-length hair. Of course she was charming enough to be spotted on the set by MGR, then reigning Tamil superstar, who wanted to cast her as his son in *Nam Naadu* (1969) directed by C.P. Jambulingam. This was Baby Sridevi's second film. Jambulingam later remade the same film in Hindi with Rajesh Khanna and Mumtaz, titled *Apna Desh* (1972). Interestingly, Sridevi's character was played by Baby Jaya Prada in the Hindi version.

In *Stardust*, October 1988 issue, Sridevi said:

> I remember the first role I played in a Telugu film was of Lord Murugan. I just did as I was told. I wasn't nervous or afraid before the camera as long as my mother was there. In those days, I used to get excited when I saw my photographs in the local magazines. I would keep looking at them over and over again. But what thrilled me even more was seeing myself larger than life, on a city hoarding at one of the market cross-roads. I ran and told all my friends in school about it. They didn't believe me at first, but soon they too saw it for themselves.
>
> Our relatives (from my father's side) didn't quite like the idea of my acting. 'How can you make your daughter a film actress', they said. My father too had some doubts. But my mother was very keen that I continue and since I seemed to enjoy it, they gradually stopped objecting. Though I must admit, at that age, I didn't quite understand what films were all about and what acting in films really meant. To be very honest, I can't recall much of my days as a child-star. Life was a routine of going to the studio, doing my make-up and giving my shot. Do you know in those days I was the only child-star to have a make-up man?[2]

Post *Thunaivan,* a year later, in *Vidhi Vilasam* (Telugu, 1970) she took a break from playing baby gods and instead played a chirpy little rich girl who lives in a bungalow and has a dog.

---

2. http://asridevi.blogspot.com/2010/10/sridevi-in-her-own-words.html

There is a funny scene in which she and another child star call out to the dog, each claiming the dog is theirs. Sridevi calls him Tommy and the other kid calls him Jackie and the poor dog is mighty confused and plonks himself halfway between the two of them (like in the game of dog and the bone; only here the humans are the dogs and the dog is the bone), thereby stealing the scene from Sridevi—a rare occurrence.

Her other big films as a child artiste in Telugu included *Maa Nanna Nirdoshi* (1970), *Badi Panthulu* (1972) and *Yashoda Krishna* (1975), in which she played Little Krishna. One by one, the films she did as a child actor would pave the way for almost a quarter-century stint in Telugu cinema.

Meanwhile, her little Lord Muruga act in Tamil films continued, like in the 1971 film *Aathi Parasakthi* in which Jayalalithaa played the role of Goddess Parvati and Gemini Ganesan was Shiva. *Agathiyar* (1972) showed Sridevi again as her favourite Lord, this time delivering complex, lengthy dialogues that an adult would have trouble with (I know she parroted her lines, but such extended monologues is no child's play). Mythology and playing versions of young gods had become her thing.

She won the Kerala State Film Award for Best Child Artist for her role as Saradha in the 1971 Malayalam movie *Poompatta* (Butterfly), which was her third Malayalam film, preceded by *Kumara Sambhavam* (1969) and *Swapnangal* (1970). In *Poompatta,* she plays the role of a long-suffering child who is orphaned and adopted by her mother's friend, but is made to live the life of a domestic worker and baby-sitter. Eventually she is 'bought' by a childless couple, but life is no bed of roses with them either.

But it was in the Tamil film *Babu* (1971) featuring Sivaji Ganesan as a rickshaw-puller that Sridevi wrenched our hearts out. An unusual bond develops between Ammu (Sridevi) and Babu (Sivaji). She is from a rich household but the family has some misfortune and they move into a hut from their palatial mansion, and Sridevi has to resort to begging, which is what she is doing when she is reunited with Babu. He later follows her to her hut where she is serving herself a humble meal of plain rice on a plantain leaf. Babu notes how much things have changed. She points to the leaf and the empty spaces around the rice and says, '*Eenge poriyal, appalam, kootu, thaiyar saadam, ooruga ... yellam nenechu pakkanam.*' (Here is poriyal, appalam, kootu, curd rice, pickle ... you have to imagine it all when you eat.)

I dare you not to cry while watching that scene.

She continued to appear as a child actor in Tamil, Telugu, Kannada and Malayalam productions. By the time Sridevi was ten, she was already a (baby) star. She would become a superstar in each of these languages as an adult.

In 2017, in an interview with Vir Sanghvi for his show *Virtuosity*, Sridevi spoke about her journey from being a child star to a heroine and doing two shifts while growing up.

> It's so strange but I didn't even realise when I became a heroine from a child artiste. One day some producers came home to meet me and all of a sudden asked my mother if I'd ever worn a saree. My mother draped me in one, thinking it is part of some get-up. The following day I was signed for *Moondru Mudichu*. The first day we reported on the sets, everyone from the spot boy to the technicians began congratulating my mother. She was puzzled, till

> someone said, 'Congratulations, your daughter has become a heroine!' I was ten and a half!

'Was this normal? You were ten and a half?' Vir Sanghvi asked her.

'I didn't know if it was normal or not. I was so grateful to them for believing in me!'

In *Anuragalu* (1975), the Telugu version of *Anuraag*, Sridevi, then eleven, was to play the role of a blind girl who becomes attached to a small child (the role Moushumi Chatterjee played in *Anuraag*). The funny thing was that the little boy she had to mother was her age! 'Both of us had a lot of fun playing and running around the studio, in between shots. The days he didn't report for shooting I'd feel very lonely and bored with nothing to do,' she said to *Stardust* years later.

Around the same time, she also played a double role, that of a mother and daughter, in a Malayalam film.

She almost never spoke about her step-brothers, except in an interview with Khalid Mohamed (*Filmfare*, 1992), when he referred to a news item in which the name of Satish Yanger, her step-brother from her father's previous marriage, had cropped up in connection with a mysterious murder in a hotel. 'That was all false, completely false. He's so simple and straightforward. He wouldn't be involved in anything remotely shady. The incident took place in the hotel where we're staying and his name was wrongly mentioned. He's a mechanical engineer and looks after our family's factory manufacturing plastic covers in Sivakasi.'

Of her childhood friends, Pinky Reddy (daughter of T. Subbarami Reddy, who produced *Chandni* and *Lamhe*) was the only one she stayed in touch with in the last few years of her life. They had grown particularly close after Pinky moved to Mumbai. When I spoke to her, Pinky recalled that as kids though, Sridevi's sister Srilatha was friendlier with her as they were closer in age; Sridevi was seven years older. She seemed unaware of any brothers in the picture, real or step. Clearly, the step-brothers were a touchy subject. 'She used to visit Nageshwar Rao, who was my neighbour, along with her parents. She had worked with him as a child artiste and her parents knew my parents. Although I have known her since childhood, it's only in the last 10-15 years, particularly the last 7-8, that we spent a lot of time together and grew really close,' said Pinky.[3]

About facing the camera for the first time, Sridevi would say to Khalid Mohamed:

> Of course, that day is so clear in my memory. I was hiding behind my mother's saree *pallu*. But she said, 'Pappi, there's nothing to be afraid of.' I believed her and that was it. I've never had a break after that. Usually, it's said that child stars have a very rough time. I didn't. But I do remember another child who was acting along with me. We had to cry for a scene and I'd just break into tears. But the other child had to be pinched hard by its mother and it would howl in pain. I played my first grown-up role at the age of eleven in the Telugu film *Anuragalu,* a remake of *Anuraag*. I was playing the blind girl and I just made my eyes go blank. I was an obedient child, I guess. I did whatever the director told me to.[4]

---

3. Interview in March 2018
4. http://sridevi.biz/filmfare-december-1992.html

She always maintained that her parents tried to keep everything 'normal'. In a cover story interview to *Good Housekeeping* (November 2007), she'd said, 'Dad made sure that I was always surrounded by family members—not to spoil or mollycoddle me but retain a "family" atmosphere. He came from a well-educated family, and being a lawyer himself, he made sure that I did not miss my education. A home tutor was always there, either on my long shoots or whenever there was a break between shootings.'[5]

In 2013, however, Sridevi spoke of missing out on a carefree childhood in an interview with *The New Indian Express*: 'I lost out on going to school and college life but I got into the film industry and worked without a gap—from child actor I went straight to heroine. There was no time to think and I was grateful for it. In order to get something you have to lose something. You can't have everything in life. So I am happy with what I got.'[6]

In 1975, in the Hindi film *Julie*, eleven-year-old Sridevi was seen grooving to Preeti Sagar's evergreen '*My heart is beating*' in hot pants; she had a demeanour that stood out even in an ensemble cast featuring top southern actress Laxmi, the powerful Nadira and Om Prakash. In another scene, as Julie (Laxmi) moans out her lover's name in her sleep, her sister Irene (Sridevi), who is lying next to her, wakes up disturbed, and yells, 'What man!'

Julie was totally out of bounds for us, and we had to make do with the sensuous songs on radio. We had heard of its

---

5. http://sridevi.biz/good-housekeeping-november-2007.html
6. https://www.khaleejtimes.com/citytimes/bollywood/i-lost-out-on-going-to-school-and-college-life-sridevi

famous lovemaking scene, the provocative clothes and its forbidden theme of 'unwed motherhood'. Years later, when I watched it on national television, I realised that Sridevi as Irene was not a child actor. She was a child-woman. I believe most Hindi movie producers noticed this too.

Sridevi had said, in an interview to *CineBlitz*, on *Julie*: 'I was eleven years old then. In the film I was supposed to have a boyfriend and I didn't even know the meaning of the word. I was so innocent then.'

Although *Julie* is widely regarded as her Hindi film debut, it was the Ashok Kumar and Vijayalalitha starrer *Rani Mera Naam* (1972) where she made her first kiddie appearance in Hindi films. It was a remake of a Telugu film, *Rowdy Rani*, and the Hindi version is only remembered for its music by R.D. Burman.

Interestingly, the very next year after *Julie* saw the release of K. Balachander's *Moondru Mudichu* (Three Knots), a Tamil film which went on to become a super hit in 1976. Sridevi co-stars with Kamal Haasan and Rajinikanth, who are roommates. Sridevi (Selvi) is in love with Kamal (Balaji), but Rajinikanth (Prasath) has his eye on her and manages to get rid of his friend by refusing to save him as he drowns after a picnic in a boat. In order to avenge his death, Selvi marries Prasath's father and uses her 'stepmother' status to indulge in the greatest power play of all time. That a twelve-year-old could pull this off is perhaps a reminder of the fact that Sridevi had grown up before her time, like most child actors do.

Kamal Haasan said in interviews he gave after her death that as child actors they grew up together, but this cannot be true because he is a good ten years older than her. When she acted opposite him in *Moondru Mudichu* in her first full-length adult role, he was already well established in Tamil films and got paid Rs 20,000 while Sridevi was given Rs 5000 and Rajinikanth, Rs 3000.

Sridevi could finally drop 'Baby' as her prefix.

It's hard to imagine whether her childhood would have been happier if she had not acted in films but just gone to school, done homework, studied for exams and played like other children. She was obviously the family's meal ticket, although she stressed time and again that there was no pressure on her to act for a living, that her father had a good practice as a lawyer, that she did it only because she enjoyed it.

Jaaved Jaaferi, dancer and actor, famously compared her to Michael Jackson in a tweet when she passed away: '#Sridevi was so much like #MichaelJackson. No childhood. Pressure to perform since a child. Always competing with own self. Extremely quiet and introverted but exploded while performing, like "that" was their life and not the one outside.' (27 February 2018)[7]

Sridevi soon transformed into the heroine the world knows her as but retained her childlike charm, possibly because she never really had a regular childhood. As a successful child star turned successful heroine, Sridevi is a rarity. She never had to sit around at home, getting over the awkward period between adolescence and adulthood. It was almost as if she went to bed a child actor one day and woke up a heroine the next.

Did Sridevi really want this? Was she happy? Did she

---

7. https://www.hindustantimes.com/bollywood/sridevi-had-no-childhood-was-always-under-pressure-to-perform-jaaved-jaaferi/story-IRfXldRuqXQ1bMhig5jlgP.html

look back on her body of work with satisfaction and not with regret? Sri was famously reticent about it all, but could it have been because she knew little else than to follow instructions, first from her parents, and then from her directors? She had been rigorously trained since the age of four to doll herself up to perfection and perform when asked. She didn't know any other way to be.

3

Amma's Girl

SRIDEVI WAS CLEARLY a by-product of an era when parents, awakened to the prospects of the 'film line', hustled their children into it aiming to make quick money, even if it involved multiple shifts, absenteeism from school and roles that ranged from the bizarre to the stupid to the plain exploitative. With each successful film, the bar of greed was raised and the question of a lost childhood inevitably swept under the carpet. The Hindi film industry was replete with young actresses who, at an impressionable age, crossed over from Dravidian lands to establish themselves in the movies of Bombay. There was a huge demand for potential heroines from Madras, who were much wanted for their big eyes, full figures and dancing skills. The heroes, however, were never much sought after.

Leading the Amma brigade was Tamil actress Vasundhara Devi, who was better known as daughter Vyjayanthimala's chaperon. As the latter's popularity soared, Amma could no longer keep her on a tight leash; Vyjayanthimala was involved in liaisons with first Dilip Kumar and then Raj Kapoor, but eventually rushed into marriage with Dr Chamanlal Bali in 1968.

Rekha's entry into Hindi cinema was also initiated by her actress mother Pushpavalli. At the age of fifteen, Rekha was a reluctant debutante, somewhat scarred by a hugely manipulated and publicised kiss with Biswajit for *Anjana Safar* (1969), her first film. She, however, adapted to the Hindi movie scene with flair in later years.

Hema Malini's mother Jaya Chakravarthy is still remembered as the most formidable 'Amma' of them all. She shadowed her daughter at the studios, but the 'Dream Girl' did end up marrying the already married Dharmendra.

'Ask Amma' was the two-worder southern lasses used a lot with potential producers and directors and even co-stars waiting to woo them. However, none of the yesteryear heroines have opened up about parental domination, except Daisy Irani, who went public about her exploitative mother, who coerced her into movies when she was only four. Irani worked multiple shifts to appear in over fifty films, including the iconic *Naya Daur* and *Dhool ka Phool,* mostly playing boys. She has suffered horrific sexual abuse as a child and she said in an interview to *Mumbai Mirror,* 'Child actors have it tough. In a majority of cases they have been taken advantage of. Maybe a few have had it easy, but most don't, really.' [1]

For Sridevi, Bollywood happened thanks to the relentless drive of her Amma, Rajeswari Yanger.

Rajeswari had aspirations to be an actress in her youth, which led her to Madras from her hometown Tirupati in Andhra Pradesh. She only played two-bit roles, sometimes as a background dancer, but her ambition never died.

---

1. https://mumbaimirror.indiatimes.com/mumbai/cover-story/the-secret-in-her-eyes/articleshow/63420165.cms

After her first husband left her, Rajeswari went to meet Ayyapan, a lawyer with a flourishing practice in Madras, to discuss her divorce. He was a married man with two sons, but he was drawn to her and wanted to help. His wife, Hamsakalyani, was perturbed by this turn of events. She thought things would change, but they changed for the worse and soon Ayyapan had moved in with Rajeswari.

Of their two daughters, Sridevi and Srilatha, Sridevi was the chosen one to make her mother's unfulfilled ambitions come true. At the age of two, she was already being made to do the rounds of the studios. Unlike other babies, she did not howl or cry when strangers picked her up, because she was used to calling them 'Mama' and 'Papa' if only for practice. The children at the tuition class that she attended on Periyar Road in Madras remember that Sridevi was always 'tip top', dressed as if she was going to a birthday party. Her mother obviously paid attention to her grooming. Schools were a waste of time for Rajeswari, who believed that music and dance were the only things Sridevi needed to know.

Maalan Narayanan reports in *Open* magazine that when she was four, Sridevi tagged along with her father (a Congress party member) to a party meeting chaired by K. Kamaraj, the veteran Congress leader.[2] He noticed this bored little child, pacing the room and gazing at the white walls lined with pictures of Gandhi and Nehru. She was getting restless. She pulled at the corner of her father's *veshti* and whispered into his ears, '*Polama*?' (Shall we go?)

Kamaraj asked Ayyapan, 'How old is she? Has she started her schooling?'

---

2. *Open*, 2 March 2108

'She will be four this August. We are trying to teach her music and dance. Her mother wants her to be a film star.'

'That's fine. But don't stop schooling her,' said Kamaraj, and turning towards Kannadasan, a popular lyricist and a party man, told him, 'Help this cute child, if you can.'

Ayyapan followed up with Kannadasan, who advised him to meet M.A. Thirumugam, a film-maker who was working on a project for legendary producer Chinnappa Thevar. So Baby Sridevi was given a small role as Lord Murugan in *Thunaivan*, and she stole the show. Posters and advertisements in the press featured her prominently. The way NTR became the image of Krishna for a Telugu audience, Sridevi became Murugan for Tamil cinemagoers. Filmmakers rushed to cash in on her charming smile and divine looks.

While her mother's dream had come true, Kamaraj's advice to her father was far from fulfilled. Sridevi did attend school and was a good student, but balancing a film career and studies proved harder than expected. Her parents even hired a teacher to accompany her when she went for shoots but films won over studies eventually.

Meanwhile, her childhood was almost in fast-forward mode, with Baby Sridevi doing two shifts a day, running from one shoot to another, doing both Tamil and Telugu films and, occasionally, Malayalam and Kannada. Before she knew it, she had turned from child to woman at the age of eleven.

That Sridevi had blossomed almost overnight did not escape the attention of her co-stars, make-up men, producers and directors. The onslaught of the male gaze turned her into a quiet, almost aloof girl. Trust didn't come easily; she hardly opened up to anyone and she had no friends. Her over-protective family (especially her mother) hovered around her all the time, keeping a close eye.

This was the period in which she did her best work in Tamil cinema with top filmmakers like J. Mahendran, P. Bharathiraja, K. Balachander and Balu Mahendra, which truly gave her the opportunity to showcase her talent and do the memorable work that Tamil film aficionados still remember her for. What her lost childhood gave us was an actor who owned every moment she appeared on screen—from the little girl who played Sivaji Ganesan's adopted daughter in the Tamil hit *Babu* (1971) to the lead heroine in *Moondru Mudichu* (1976).

But, sadly, there was a lot of exploitative work that makes one wonder how it passed muster with her parents. Like the song from I.V. Sasi's *Pagalil Oru Iravu* where a fifteen-year-old Sridevi appears in a shredded skirt (she has ripped off a piece to bandage her co-star's forehead). In the song, the actor (a much older Ravikumar) is so taken in by her that he deflowers her in the open fields, blades of grass camouflaging the act. We only know what's happening as the camera pans across his face and hers, as they orgasm. The fact that this was done to Ilaiyaraaja's music doesn't make it less barfworthy.

It is hard to believe that her mother was present at the shoot while the song was being filmed.

On screen Sridevi was suddenly romancing the very men she had played a child or grandchild to just a few years ago, including N.T. Rama Rao, A. Nageswara Rao, Krishna and others. Still a child inside, she was all-woman to the world. All she needed to do was make big eyes and bite her lower lip.

When I was a child, Sridevi hadn't yet made it to Hindi cinema and my mother considered Tamil movies like *Moondru Mudichu, 16 Vayathinile* and just about any film she did with

Kamal Haasan or Rajinikanth inappropriate for children (and they were, with innuendos and subtexts). I was able to watch them only in my late teens. So I was horrified to learn that she was only twelve when she did *Moondru Mudichu*. The plot was complex even for an adult, but to imagine she was still a child when she shot for it! *16 Vayathinile* was filmed when she was fourteen and she played a nineteen-year-old who was sexually exploited. There is a scene in this P. Bharathiraja film where she is seen raising her *paavadai* (lehenga) for the viewing pleasure of a creepy pervert. I can't help but be horrified at her mother's decision to put her daughter through this.

After her terrific innings in Telugu and Tamil films, Jeetendra who was by then being wooed by Padmalaya Film Studios and other Telugu production houses, expressed interest in Sridevi acting in *Himmatwala* (a remake of Telugu's *Ooruki Monagadu)*. Her mother was more than happy as she knew it was time to raise the bar and the Bombay film industry was the right leg up. She knew the same formula—of successful hero-heroine pairing—would be repeated if *Himmatwala* was a success. Since it was, Sridevi was set for another dozen films with Jeetendra.

Things were working as per plan. There were a few preparations required though. Her perky nose, which had so charmed her fans in the south, had to be mainstreamed into a straight one. Grooming lessons in clothes, hair and make-up ensured she was more acceptable to audiences in the north to whom she was unfamiliar. Perhaps Sridevi was overwhelmed by the burdens of her youthful beauty and the ensuing male gaze, and producers' constant demands to put her in titillating song-and-dance sequences in one remake after another.

However, her life had become all about pleasing Amma and Appa so she acquiesced to it all.

It was only in Bombay that Sridevi, the bird in the gilded cage, slowly learned to spread her wings a bit. Although she travelled on shoots with her entourage—her mother or sister was always by her side, and stayed at the same five-star hotel—Sri did find the time to fall in love.

It happened in 1983, on the sets of *Jaag Utha Insaan*, when Mithun took her under his wing.[3] He was a breath of fresh air, and they were soon deeply involved, although he was a married man with children. This liaison upset her mother. Sridevi had just struck gold in Bollywood, and had a long way to go. Marriage and love had no place in the busy schedule of her Pappi (Sridevi's pet name). So mamma Yanger called a ban on all films with the Bengali babu, thereby reducing opportunities for them to meet or hang out.

In the mid-1980s, Mithun was a really busy star. Their pairing was a hit and her fans were glad to see her with someone other than Jeetendra. However, apart from the three films they had on the floor (*Guru, Watan ke Rakhwale* and *Waqt ke Shehzade*), there was to be no more. Mithun let her go quite easily and went back to his wife.

Sridevi's mother always accompanied her to shoots, making sure her daughter stayed away from the bad boys and men on the sets. Rajeswari Yanger masterminded her career: the films she did, whom she worked with, her call sheets, the schedule, the script, the money. Sridevi did read the scripts,

3. 'Dark Secrets', *Stardust*, April 2011

but it was always her mother who took the final call. Every move was carefully planned. The media had by then already painted Sridevi as part of 'those actresses from the south with dubious mothers' squad. Rajeswari was finally seeing the limelight through her daughter, and she was thrilled by the heights Sridevi had reached.

Her father's death in 1991 left Sridevi shattered. This was compounded further by her mother's failing health. A botched-up operation at Memorial Sloan Kettering Cancer Center, one of the world's premier hospitals, in New York City, sealed her fate. On 26 May 1995, the fifty-nine-year-old Rajeswari underwent surgery for a malignant tumour on the left side of her brain. The tumour, however, was left intact because the neurosurgeon operated on the wrong side of her brain, turning the woman who managed Sridevi's career into an invalid. 'My mother used to handle my properties, my affairs, my taxes, my career,' Sridevi told her New York lawyer Harvey Wachsman, when she was suing the hospital. 'Now she is like a vegetable,' she added.[4] The death of her parents, who had worked relentlessly to make her a star loved by millions, left her alone.

It also taught her to make place for love, and she finally married Boney Kapoor in 1996, at the age of thirty-three.

Soon after, Sridevi won ₹7.10 crore in a compensation suit against the US hospital. Her sister, Srilatha Ramaswamy, then took the family to court to settle the dispute over sharing the compensation and other family property. They soon reached a compromise, however, facilitated by Boney Kapoor.

---

4. *Open*, 2 March 2018

4

Language No Bar

IN THE BITTERSWEET comedy *English Vinglish* released in 2012, Sridevi plays an Indian housewife (Shashi) who sneaks off to an English class while in New York for her niece's wedding, so she can win some respect from her family. In the first class, when she is asked to introduce herself in English by her teacher, David, she stutters and mutters and explains that she is from 'The India' and runs a small business from home, making snacks called 'laddoos'. To which her teacher says, 'We have an entrepreneur!'

He goes on to spell the word on the board.

Shashi's expression slowly changes from curiosity to awe as she takes in this big word, breaking it up phonetically as 'on-tre-pre-noor' over and over, trying to say it to herself till she gets it right. As she walks down the street after class, her body language slowly transforms from hesitant to confident and then, in the manner of having conquered the world, she breaks into a dance, Michael Jackson-style, on the pavements of New York. She has had the realisation that she is, after all, a person with worth, English or no English.

Cut to *Sadma* (1983) in which school teacher Somu

(Kamal Haasan) and Nehalata/Reshmi (Sridevi), whom he has just rescued from a brothel in Bombay, have taken a train and are now walking through the wilderness of Ooty to his home. She is gazing up at the tall, imposing trees around her in this new landscape in total bewilderment.

'*Yeh kya hai, kitna bada hai*?' (What are these things, so big and tall?) she asks, pointing at the trees.

'Oh that! Eucalyptus,' Kamal replies.

'You ... Kya?' she tries to repeat, befuddled by this mouthful.

He smiles and breaks it down for her, enunciating every syllable, recognising that she is after all a six-year-old trapped in the body of a woman.

'You-ca-lip-tus.'

She repeats it over and over, still far from getting it, but feeling good she tried.

And that was the thing about Sridevi and language. When she said things over and over, even in a language she didn't understand, she was ultimately able to wing it. Or we chose not to notice even if she didn't (like when she said '*yinkaar*' instead of '*inkaar*' in *Gurudev* or '*womeed*' instead of '*umeed*' in *Gumrah*). When Sridevi spoke, it was not just the words you heard. Her eyes spoke, her face spoke, every wobble of her lips spoke. Her entire being spoke. Language was incidental.

When I watched Sridevi's earlier films, it did rankle that the words were not coming out right. Her voice got in the way. Her accent was too 'Madrasi' as people north of the Vindhyas would typify all south Indians, whether their mother tongue was Tamil, Telugu, Kannada or Tamil. We were known as the '*andugundus*', and it annoyed me no end. As a south Indian growing up in a cosmopolitan neighbourhood, but with chiefly north Indians as neighbours—the Kakkars and the Malviyas—I had a point to prove. That all 'Madrasis' didn't speak 'like that'.

I was used to Rekha's *'khhoomaars'* and *'khhatas'* from the epiglottis by then. And so I set out to master the language and did, with a little help from Sahir and Majrooh and Gulzar's lyrics and also by mimicking Rekha, who in turn was mimicking her tall beau, unbeknownst to me.

My mother, of course, didn't give a damn, and spoke Hindi exactly as it suited her, even though, by then, it had been close to two decades since she had left her hometown, Bangalore, and moved to Bombay.

In *Khuda Gawah,* Sridevi played a double role: one avatar was of an independent, free-spirited Afghan woman and the other was of her lookalike daughter, who travels to India in search of her father. She is a Pathan who speaks with a south Indian accent (perhaps the first south Indian Pathan), but then her charisma and spunk overrode her lack of language skills. When Mehndi (Sridevi) gets into an intense discussion with her foster father Khuda Baksh (Danny) over betrayal and loyalty and trust and integrity, it no longer mattered to me that an Afghan was speaking with a strange accent. When she says, '*Lale di jaan*', (a term of endearment) to a passing car driver as she zips around in her rally, it mattered even less.

In *Meri Biwi ka Jawab Nahin* (2004), she speaks Hindi with a Bhojpuri accent, often in couplets, as she plays the local housewife-spy, spotting goons and taking them to task.

Her '*mood banana ko*' in a Hyderabadi accent in *Gurudev* is a delight. Nothing was off limits. She was good at learning lines and delivering them, even if she didn't understand what she was saying.

Sridevi had turned her language handicap into a quirk. Throughout her Hindi film career, she spoke Hindi with a thick, sing-song Tamil accent, and depending on whether one is a Sridevi fan or not, this could be grating or cute. For Jerry Pinto, author of the national award-winning *Helen: The Life and Times of a Bollywood H-Bomb*, it was grating. In an interview to me, he said:

> For better or worse, Hindi cinema has always had a love affair with Urdu. (This may be dying now since Bollywood is having a fling with Punjabi.) You had to be able to deliver your dialogue right in order to be a contender. Whether it was *Mughal-e Azam* or *Sholay*, dialogue mattered because it was what we carried away in our minds, what we deployed when we spoke, how we expressed in an emotional shorthand what we felt. '*Dost dost na rahaa*,' you might say in a moment of betrayal; or you might call a boss, Mogambo. Now here was a woman who did not speak her own dialogue. Someone dubbed it for her. The artificiality of this made the artificiality of the whole enterprise much more grating and there was already enough to grate on one's nerves. (Does anyone remember how much in demand the Shakti Kapoor-Kader Khan pairing was?) So '*De mortuis nil nisi bonum*' and all that, but no, I was not a fan.[1]

1. Email sent in March 2018

Sridevi's language barrier led to a certain guardedness or aloofness on sets, which people construed as arrogance. However, it kept her away from unnecessary chatter and gossip, and that remained with her all her life. All through the 1980s, when her career was at an all-time high, she was a fortress that journalists could not breach. She spoke very little and mostly answered in monosyllables. The media was also not very kind to her. They called her 'thunder thighs' and 'ask Mummy' because most of her answers were either 'ask Mummy' or 'yes' or 'no'.

When Hindi movie directors briefed her, they wondered if she really understood them, because she would often have a blank expression on her face. But the minute the camera was on, she transformed into a live wire, an *apsara*, in the way she danced and did her scenes. She was a master at facing the camera even though she didn't understand a word of the language.

In his memoir, *Khullam Khulla,* Rishi Kapoor refers to his language barrier issues with Sridevi. 'She may have looked arrogant, but that was due to the language problem. Slowly, down the years, she started conversing.'[2]

It was during the shoot of *Nagina* (blockbuster of 1986) that Kapoor had one of his most embarrassing encounters with Sridevi. They were shooting a song when the magazine of the camera ran out and they had no option but to remain locked in each other's arms till the magazine was refilled and the camera started rolling again. In those extremely awkward moments, Sridevi told him, 'Sir, I have seen *Khel Khel Mein* four

2. Interview in *India Today*, 2018, https://www.indiatoday.in/movies/celebrities/story/rishi-kapoor-on-sridevi-1178346-2018-02-27

times.' Rishi, with whom Sri had only exchanged greetings till that point, was shocked. It was one of the only conversations they would have while working on the film.

It was finally during the making of *Chandni* that their relationship would move beyond the usual 'namaste' and 'good night'. She developed a casual, almost playful, ease with him—a far cry from her usual reclusive self. Rishi Kapoor gives credit to Sridevi for making some of the scenes from the film memorable: these were actually improvised on set. Like the ice-cream scene in Switzerland in which Sridevi asks for a lick of his ice-cream and takes a nice big bite, but when it's his turn, she shows him her thumb and says, '*Thenga!*'

Chandni, 1989

'They used to call me a "parrot". I used to mug lines, the meaning and giving the expression, without knowing the language. I'd retain the dialogue, emote what was necessary, but I didn't know what I was saying in the beginning when I did films in Kannada, Malayalam and even in Hindi in the 1980s. Now I'm better but ...,' she had said during an interview to CNN at the Toronto International Film Festival where *English Vinglish* was screened.[3] 'I've always had a problem with language—I'm not fluent in any. So when I did this film (*English Vinglish*), I could relate to it instantly.'

Sridevi's multilingualism may also explain why when she was asked what had changed in Bollywood during her absence since 1997, the first thing she mentioned was the improved technology, especially the use of synchronised sound. Traditionally, Bollywood producers added the soundtrack post production; voice tracks recorded on set using sync sound have come into vogue only in the last decade.

'After the film, you would go to the theatre and dub. When the performance is emotional, or in comedy where timing is of essence, it's very difficult to get the same effect,' she had said. 'The sync sound: That really helps an actor to retain the spontaneity of the performance.'[4]

It is said that when Sridevi first came to Bollywood, it was Rekha who took her under her wing and mentored her. When Rekha herself came to Bombay, she didn't know the language

---

3. https://www.theglobeandmail.com/arts/film/sridevi-fluent-in-sounding-fluent-onscreen/article4591679/

4. https://www.theglobeandmail.com/arts/film/sridevi-fluent-in-sounding-fluent-onscreen/article4591679/

or the people. However, after the initial gawky years, she mastered the language with such flair she could even sing in Hindi (remember '*Qayda qayda*' in *Khoobsoorat*?). But she was the exception and not the rule. Hema Malini was still stuck at her cry of '*Nahinnnnn*' and Jaya Prada called Amitabh '*Weaky Babu*' in *Sharaabi*.

Over a period of time, Rekha and Sridevi became good friends and continued to support each other's work. 'I find that the industry women are very hypocritical towards me. Because I don't know English and Hindi very well, they always try to show that they are one up on me. Rekha is the only one who is different. She's a very warm, caring and sensitive person. And she's my only friend and critic,' Sridevi had said in an interview to *CineBlitz* in August 1985.[5]

Speaking about Sridevi, Rekha had said, 'I've always loved that girl. She had a special spark about her. I believe after Vyjanthimala and Hema Malini, Sridevi was the third Tamil superstar in Hindi cinema.' She added, 'I don't think I was anywhere near these actresses!'[6]

Born to a Tamil father and a Telugu mother, Sridevi never faced any problems in speaking the two languages in her films. That left Malayalam and Hindi. At the start of her career in Hindi films, her parts used to get dubbed, initially by prominent actresses and later by a noted child actress of the past, Naaz, who dubbed quite a few Sridevi films and had got her pitch and sing-song voice down pat. Rekha dubbed for her

---

5. http://www.freepressjournal.in/entertainment/i-was-a-very-shy-and-lonely-child-sridevi/646895

6. https://www.deccanchronicle.com/entertainment/bollywood/040318/rekhas-no-led-to-sridevis-stardom.html

Aakhree Raasta, 1986

in *Aakhree Raasta*. Revathy dubbed some of her Malayalam films.

For *Janbaaz* (1986), Feroz Khan insisted that she dub her own lines. This was rare and unusual for a Sridevi film. Since it was a small part, she agreed. This set the stage for Yash Chopra's *Chandni*, where she dubbed her own lines in the entire movie and then she never went back to a dubbing artiste. Sridevi even sang in *Chandni*, but as a singer she was still being Sridevi with her sing-song, girly voice. However, this was lauded by many, including her co-star Rishi Kapoor in his autobiography.

In 1983, just before the release of *Himmatwala*, Jeetendra had told film journalist and historian Bhawana Somaaya, 'Just watch her; she doesn't speak a word in Hindi but she is going to be a sensation in Bombay after this film.'[7] Perhaps acting, like music, doesn't need a language and when we imported Sridevi from the south, we knew that even though she couldn't speak either Hindi or English, that fact didn't hamper her acting at all.

When Shekhar Kapur was briefing her on the '*I love you*' song in *Mr India* (1987), she would listen to him and translate his lines into Tamil, repeating them to her sister Srilatha standing next to her.[8] Shekhar knew it was her way of processing his ideas and instructions. Srilatha shadowed Sridevi everywhere, video camera in hand, shooting her dance sequences, her expressions, her every move. At night, they watched the results together, working on improving the visuals and, unobtrusively, Sridevi perfected it.

Pankaj Parashar, who directed Sridevi in *ChaalBaaz* (1989), spoke about his first meeting with Sridevi in an interview to Nandini Ramnath of Scroll.in: 'Poornachandra Rao had fixed up a meeting with Sridevi. She was shooting for a film, and had on a feather boa and blue contact lenses. She said, tell me your story. I hadn't written anything down. I narrated the plot of *Seeta aur Geeta* from the beginning till the end. She looked at Poornachandra and said in Telugu, "I am in".'

---

7. https://theprint.in/opinion/she-doesnt-speak-hindi-but-will-be-a-sensation-sridevi-was-a-star-unlike-any-other/37974/
8. *Stardust*, March 1988

In the same interview,[9] he goes on to say that he later confessed to Sridevi that what he had narrated to her was the script of *Seeta aur Geeta,* not *ChaalBaaz,* and she told him she knew that, and then said that she had watched *Jalwa* on a video cassette. 'I know you know exactly what you are doing; don't worry, it will be different.'

ChaalBaaz, 1989

'On the first few days of the shoot, Sridevi was distant,' said Parasher. 'She wouldn't talk much, and we could not communicate. We used to talk through her make-up man or

9. https://theprint.in/opinion/she-doesnt-speak-hindi-but-will-be-a-sensation-sridevi-was-a-star-unlike-any-other/37974/

her assistant. Then I showed her the rushes of what we had shot, and from that moment on, she was a totally different human being. She looked at me and smiled and said, this is good. From then on, we became a team.'

He went on to say, 'I would throw something at her, and she would throw something at me, and that's how the film grew.'

ChaalBaaz, 1989

ChaalBaaz, which to me is still Sridevi's finest movie, is a whacked-out comedy with plenty of pop culture references and peppy music. Parasher took the oft-repeated formula of identical twins separated at birth and gave it an exaggerated, comic-book treatment. Sridevi plays the demure, God-fearing, oppressed Anju and the street-smart, beer-loving Manju. She won a Filmfare award for best actress in 1989 (her first in Hindi cinema) for this film.

There is a scene in the movie in which she imitates actor Raaj Kumar while threatening Amba (Rohini Hattangadi) with a knife. That line and that scene— *'Jaani yeh chaku hai lag jaye to khoon nikal aata hain'*—have gone down in history as one of the most iconic comic scenes ever in Indian cinema.

When I spoke to Rauf Ahmed, author of *Shammi Kapoor: The Game Changer* and ex-editor of *Filmfare,* he felt that language didn't really matter in Sridevi's case, because barring *Lamhe,* her movies never really had that depth of dialogue that was characteristic of the earlier decades of Hindi cinema.

> It was not like she had to deliver heavy dialogues like those of Meena Kumari. Of the south Indian heroines, Vyjayanthi was the only one who was consistent with working on her dialogue, but then she had a tutor in Dilip Kumar. She mastered the language, delivered intense dialogues and was a great dancer. Hema Malini never learnt Hindi—but she never got those great roles, so it didn't matter then either. Rekha mastered the language because she was a great mimic and developed a flair for it, but she wasn't really in the reckoning for the top heroine slot as she was inconsistent. Every now and then, she would take off.

While her rival Jaya Prada tried to improve her Hindi game by hiring a Urdu tutor to give her diction lessons, Sridevi did no such thing. For *Nagina,* she had Naaz. *Nagina* became the fluke blockbuster of 1986, and changed the game for Sridevi, who had the last (shrill) laugh. In this film, no one cared about her language skills (or lack thereof) or her diction. People couldn't really expect the character of a cobra woman to speak in Ghalib's Urdu, could they?

Poonam Saxena, editor of *Hindustan Times Sunday Magazine* and co-author of *An Unsuitable Boy*, Karan Johar's memoir, doesn't think Sridevi's 'language problem' was a problem at all. She told me:

> In fact, there have been so many actresses in the past who spoke really bad Hindi, but they never came under the scanner. Sharmila Tagore in *Kashmir ki Kali* spoke with a thick Bengali accent, referring to *bhagwan* (God) as *bhogwon*. So did Rakhee throughout her career. Even Hema Malini never learnt Hindi and it never bothered anyone. They all ended up being top actresses.
>
> And, honestly, it doesn't matter because Hindi film audiences are largely forgiving. All they need is a film they can emotionally connect with. She definitely made that connection with the audience. She made them fall in love with her.[10]

For someone who always had a language dilemma, Sridevi had a long and illustrious career across almost three hundred Hindi, Telugu, Tamil, Malayalam and Kannada movies. She established that connection through her expressive face, even though her words may not always have had the perfect diction. In her climactic speech in *English Vinglish*, as she raises a toast at her niece's wedding, her character Shashi says, 'Life is a long journey ... sometimes you will feel you are less [than

---

10. Interview in April 2018

the other]. Try to help each other—to feel equal ... [But sometimes] you have to help yourself. Nobody can help you better than you. If you do that, you will return back feeling equal ... Your life will be beautiful.'

And, in some small way, with all her linguistic imperfections, she did make many lives beautiful. Three hours at a time.

5

Our Sridevi, Their Sridevi

SRIDEVI WAS NOT entirely pleased that her first big hit in Hindi cinema was *Himmatwala* ('The Brave One') in 1983. In an interview with Raj Chengappa of *Business Today* in 1987, she spoke of her image as a sex siren in Hindi films and how differently the Tamil film industry perceived her. It felt as though my mother had written the script for that interview.

'In Tamil films they love to see me act naturally. But in Hindi films all they want is a lot of glamour, richness and masala. My bad luck was that my first big hit in Hindi films turned out to be a commercial one (*Himmatwala*). When I did a character role in *Sadma,* the picture flopped. So people started casting me only for glamour roles. But one day I'm going to prove to everyone that I can act also.'[1]

She did.

Soon after, *Mr India* was released and it was a movie that offered a 70mm range for her versatility as an actress—she played a Lois Lane-like reporter who conveyed it all. Whether

---

1. https://www.businesstoday.in/trending/entertainment/remembering-sridevi-i-am-an-ordinary-person-just-another-parents-daughter/story/271435.html

it was her comic timing or her Chaplinesque routine or her song-and-dance bonanza—from '*Hawa Hawai*' to '*I love you*', where she took sensuality several notches higher in a blue chiffon sari, but without a hint of vulgarity. *Mr India* was the year's best film and a riot at the box office; it had something for everyone, and was one of her most loveable performances. Sridevi had finally proved to Hindi cinema that she was more than just a box office draw.

Mr India, 1987

Sridevi had that pan-Indian appeal, which is tough to achieve in a country with twenty-three official languages, several film industries and diverse regional cultures. In a curious contradiction of sorts, Sridevi, who had a language and communication problem, ended up working in several regional cinemas: Hindi, Tamil, Telugu, Kannada and Malayalam. She was one of the first crossover stars in Indian cinema (perhaps the most successful one), who shone wherever she went. She didn't let language get in the way, nor was she bothered by the cultural milieus, or the quality of the films.

If you consider the sheer volume and quality of her work, and the durability she had as a top star (for over fifteen years, if you count her southern innings) across industries in different languages, you'd see that Sridevi had accomplished the unthinkable. In the largely male-dominated Indian film industry, no matter what language she worked in, she made her mark. None of her leading men or contemporary heroines have had the breadth of her impact and range.

Over the course of her career, she made eighty-three films in Telugu, seventy-two in Hindi, seventy-one in Tamil, twenty-three in Malayalam, and six in Kannada. (Boney Kapoor claimed *Mom* was her 300th film but it doesn't add up. Maybe 300 is a good number. May be it was important for the marketing of the film.)

Through the 1970s, '80s and until the mid-'90s, Sridevi shifted seamlessly between different languages and industries, holding her own amongst the heavyweights. Perhaps the fact that the '80s (Sridevi's super-stardom years) was a time when the Telugu, Tamil and Hindi film industries worked quite closely together had something to do with this. If a film was a hit in one language, it was remade into another and yet another. Most often it made sense to work with the same star. So when Sridevi's *16 Vayathinile* (with Kamal Haasan and Rajinikanth) in Tamil became a hit, it was remade in Telugu (*Padaharella Vayasu*) and then in Hindi (*Solva Sawan*), and later in Malayalam. The lead male actors were different in each language, but Sridevi remained a constant. P. Bharathiraja had directed her in the Tamil and Hindi versions, while the Telugu version was directed by K. Raghavendra Rao.

16 Vayathinile, 1977

Bharathiraja said in an interview to *Firstpost* in February 2018, soon after her death:

> There are a lot of actresses who forayed into Bollywood and other industries and disappeared without a trace. But Sridevi was an exception. She ruled all the film industries during her heyday. Today, I can proudly say that I'm the one who introduced her in Bollywood through *Solva Sawan* where she shared the screen with Amol Palekar. When I told her about the remake idea, she was skeptical and refused to

> set foot in Hindi cinema. Then I promised her that I would take care of everything and convinced her to do the film. She later climbed up the ladder of Bollywood through her relentless hard work and extraordinary talent.

It would be pointless to turn the discussion on Sridevi's legacy into a Bolly/Kolly/Tolly/Mollywood one. Each industry believed Sridevi was 'theirs'. But who was the real Sridevi? For fans, there are several Sridevis. There is the Sridevi of *Moondram Pirai* and *16 Vayathinile* in Tamil Nadu. For another kind of Tamil movie buff, there is the Sridevi of *Johnny, Priya* and *Guru*. The choices are between *Vazhve Maayam* and *Varumayin Niram Sivappu*. Or *Sigappu Rojakkal* and *Meendum Kokila*. Or *Karthika* Deepama and *Kshana Kshanam*. Or *Mr India* and *ChaalBaaz*. *Lamhe* and *Chandni*. Come to think of it, even *Roop Ki Rani Choron Ka Raja* has fans.

But as a south Indian born and raised in Bombay and fortified on Hindi cinema, mine was still a household where my parents (especially my mother) missed the cinema of their land, their youth, and had trouble reconciling to Hindi cinema. Having seen Sridevi's best in Tamil, Hindi was, at best, a consolation; at worst a dilution of her flair and craft. My mother was hugely underwhelmed with what little she saw, and refused to see the rest.

In our home, it was never a Madhuri vs Sridevi debate, but rather a Sri in Bombay vs a Sri in the south debate between my parents. When I started watching Sridevi films from the early '80s and '90s, I watched her Bollywood hits before I watched her work in Tamil. So initially I could not quite figure out why Amma used to keep insisting that Sri was way better in Tamil movies and was wasted in Bombay (*Sadma, Mr India, Chandni,*

ChaalBaaz and *Lamhe* being the only exceptions). But even I was frankly aghast at her roles in films like *Mawaali, Maqsad, Masterji, Tohfa, Mr Bechara, Chandra Mukhi* and *Chaand Kaa Tukdaa.* Some of her movies had a so-bad-they-were-good feel to them, but the rest of them didn't even deserve to be made fun of.

Later, when I watched her older Tamil and Malayalam movies, I could see what Amma meant. This is not taking away from some of her best roles in Bollywood—it is just that if one were to analyse her range of performances, her finest did lie in the south.

TAMIL

In Tamil cinema Sridevi was this cute, innocent girl with all her subtle nuances. She worked under great directors who told beautiful stories and she managed to make her mark alongside the big names of the time. She was part of that golden period when Tamil cinema celebrated the complete range of histrionics of three of its rising stars: Sridevi, Kamal Haasan and Rajinikanth.

Even as she moved from child actor to young child-woman, the roles she took on were complex and nuanced; of course, she looked mature beyond her years while playing them. *Moondru Mudichu, 16 Vayathinile, Sigappu Rojakkal, Johnny, Meendum Kokila, Moondram Pirai, Varumayin Niram Sigappu*—she played layered and complex roles in them all, and she wasn't even twenty!

It was also a special time in Tamil cinema when the writing and storytelling veered away from the melodramatic of the earlier decade to create moods and textures that were typical of

16 Vayathinile, 1977

filmmakers like K. Balachander, J. Mahendran, P. Bharathiraja and Balu Mahendra, all of whom she worked with. Much was written about the Sridevi-Kamal 'romantic fit' on screen—they had a light, easy chemistry, there was almost an organic understanding between the two. They understood each other's eye movements and body language; this perhaps was because they were both child actors who grew up to be stars and acting had, by then, become second nature to them.

The Kamal-Sridevi pair delivered a number of iconic blockbuster films, like *Kalyanaraman*, where she plays the young estate worker Shenbagam who loses her mind when she sees her lover being killed. In *Sigappu Rojakkal* she is an innocent young sales girl who falls in love with and marries the rich, debonair Kamal only to discover he is a serial killer. She kept audiences on the edge of their seats as she found out the truth and tried to escape as Kamal stalked her and finally murdered her as well.

Their chemistry is epitomised in the song '*Sippi irukkudu muthum irukkudu*' in *Varumaiyin Niram Sivappu* ('Poverty Is a Shade of Red', 1980), where Sridevi's scat-verses are lifted by Kamal into words and you can't get enough of this exchange. The duo pulled it off with such élan that singer S.P. Balasubrahmanyam (who lent the male voice for the song) later said that this was the song that came closest to the actors looking like real singers on screen.

In *Meendum Kokila* (1981), the duo displayed a fine sense of comedy. Sridevi plays the coy Iyengar maami who is insecure about her husband's crush on an actress (played by Deepa), while Kamal plays the man caught between two women, with a great sense of comic timing.

And the songs! Who can forget their songs together? '*Devi Sridevi*' from *Vaazhve Maayam* (1982), '*Radha Radha nee enge*' from *Meendum Kokila* (1981) in which Kamal is the goofy Krishna in a silver jacket with a peacock-feathered fedora, and Sridevi matches him step for step (he, a trained Bharatanatyam dancer, and she, just a girl who loved to dance).

Of course, the definitive movie for the pair has to be

Moondram Pirai (it was the original version of *Sadma,* the film which started the whole Sridevi thing between my mother and me). As the adorably amnesic Viji (Bhagyalakshmi), Sridevi literally walked into the hearts of the Tamil audience and resided there for a long time. It's no wonder that my mother was hung up on her performance after all those years. Kamal Haasan won the National Award for *Moondram Pirai,* which was well deserved; Sridevi, however, missed on something equally deserving.

Then there was the Sridevi-Kamal-Rajini trio in *Moondru Mudichu* and, later, in *16 Vayathinile,* which was a hit and launched several careers and won several awards. It is celebrated as the first realistic portrayal of rural life in commercial cinema. The Telugu version (*Padaharella Vayasu*) was a hit too, but the Hindi version (*Solva Sawan*) flopped badly.

The Rajini-Sridevi duo had a different kind of magic, even when they didn't star opposite each other. In the movies in which they did—*Dharma Yuddham, Johnny, Ranuva Veeran, Pokkiri Raja, Thanikattu Raja, Adutha Varisu* and *Gaayathri*—there was a great sense of balance between the two, their energies well-matched.

They appeared together as husband and wife in *Gaayathri,* where Rajini plays the perverted husband who makes blue films featuring his wife. However, their best collaboration as a couple was in *Johnny,* which shows the quiet, unspoken love between singer Archana (Sridevi) and Johnny (Rajinikanth). This was among Sridevi's best performances in Tamil cinema as well.

As film critic Baradwaj Rangan explains in his article for 'Film Companion', a popular website on Indian cinema:

> Perhaps her greatest gift was that she gave each director what they wanted. If Bharathiraja, in *16 Vayathinile* (1977), wanted her to do nothing more than stand still, conveying sadness through her eyes (they were big, beautiful eyes) as his camera zoomed in, she did that. If Balachander, in *Varumayin Niram Sivappu* (1980), wanted her to mimic S. Janaki's wordless musical phrases in the '*Sippi irukkuthu*' song sequence, she did that—she was a marvellous 'song performer', which is its own kind of acting. And she did what S.P. Muthuraman asked of her in *Adutha Varisu* (1983), where Rajinikanth tries to pass her off as the heiress to a province. The sceptical queen quizzes her about the state symbol. She throws her head back and laughs exaggeratedly (she's saying, through that laugh, 'Surely you don't expect me to not know the answer to this!'), buying time till Rajinikanth gestures to the lion carving above the queen's throne. She collects herself and gives the right answer.[2]

Sridevi had pretty much reached her peak in Tamil cinema or, rather, Tamil cinema had reached its peak in offering her what she deserved; there was a marked shift post the mid-eighties as far as the treatment of heroines went. It morphed into a male-centric, superstar-driven industry, where all the great actresses of the time had no choice but to recede into playing the shadow of the hero. Sridevi's exit from the south (especially Tamil cinema) coincided with a dwindling of that wonderful era of filmmaking. Movies became more action-oriented or were crass comedies. Women were reduced to props for their male counterparts, and hardly any roles were written for then,

2. https://www.filmcompanion.in/sridevi-kapoor-death-obituary/

except perhaps *Sindhu Bhairavi* by K. Balachander or Mani Ratnam's memorable *Mouna Ragam.*

Amma was in denial of all this; she believed that amid the Bollywood glitz, Sridevi had lost interest in Tamil films. This was not so. Sridevi's last film in Tamil in that period was *Naan Adimai Illai* (1986) with Rajinikanth. The movie, a remake of Mithun Chakraborty's *Pyar Jhukta Nahin,* evoked mixed feelings in Sridevi buffs from the south. I remember Amma discussing the film with her sisters and then deciding not to see it. 'How can she do this to us? Why did she desert us to go to Hindi movies? And that too to sing and dance with that Jeetendra?'

The Sridevi-Rajini pairing and camaraderie looked alien in the film. Because, by then, Sridevi was well and truly a Bollywood diva.

Even if the earlier era of narrative-driven films had continued, I don't think Tamil cinema would have allowed Sridevi the chance to outshine her male co-stars. She would probably have had to play second fiddle to Kamal/Rajini. Perhaps the timing of her foray into Hindi cinema was perfect. But how do you go from *Moondram Pirai* to *Himmatwala,* people wondered. Sridevi, though, had the last laugh and in the process also discovered her comic timing.

We can argue that Bollywood didn't deserve her, or that she was light years ahead of the films they cast her in but she gave them what they asked for, adding that extra dash of something that made her performances such a delight to watch. Amma's Sridevi had become 'their' Sridevi.

MALAYALAM

Sridevi acted in around twenty-three Malayalam films—the first in 1969 when she appeared in *Kumara Sambhavam* as the trident-holding baby Lord Kartikeya, the son of Shiva-Parvati. In 1971, film buffs in Kerala had seen her in *Poompatta* (Butterfly) in which plays a sweet little girl oppressed by domesticity even as she has aspirations to study in school. The film won her a Kerala State Film Award for Best Child Artist. By 1976, Sridevi (only thirteen) had morphed into a butterfly and played her first adult role in the Malayalam film *Thulavarsham,* in which she swings down a tree from her two-storeyed house to rendezvous with her lover with whom she sings a song by a lake.

This was followed by *Oonjaal* (Swing, 1977), directed by I.V. Sasi in which Sridevi played the quintessential *naadan*. She was the archetypal countryside girl in mundu-veshti—effusive, flowers in her hair, swinging in a coconut-palm orchard with a group of girls, some of whom are later seen bathing in an open pond. When a local toughie declares to her that only he would wed her, she responds demurely, her head hanging, as she would act in the company of any man. She was the girl-next-door, and Keralites believed she was actually a Malayali. Her inability to speak the language was not an issue, as dubbing was a common practice.

Around the same time, Hindi cinema had noticed her in *Julie* (directed by K.S. Sethumadhavan) starring Lakshmi as a free-spirited Anglo-Indian girl, Julie, who falls in love with a Hindu boy, Shashi (Vikram). Sridevi plays Irene, Lakshmi's audacious little sister.

She did show up in a couple of Kerala movies in the '80s, but that was it. In 1996 she made an appearance in Bharathan's

Devaraagam with Arvind Swamy. In the movie she portrays a woman caught in an unusual dilemma—married against her will to a man who is impotent and who insists she keep the child she conceived with her lover before she married him, because he wants the world to think it is his. Sridevi transitions from a wide-eyed, flirtatious young maiden to a worn-out, devastated mother, in a fine performance. The film was a huge flop though, perhaps because for the Malayali audience, Sridevi had become a 'Hindi actress' by then.

TELUGU

If Tamil gave Sridevi range and great co-stars and Malayalam gave her early critical appreciation, Telugu films were a true glam fest. Telugu was also her mother tongue and a language she did the maximum number of movies in. Around the time she was winning accolades for her acting chops in Tamil and Malayalam films, she was also playing arm candy (albeit a hugely successful one) to actors like N.T. Rama Rao or Akkineni Nageswara Rao (famously known as NTR and ANR)—actors who sported wigs, make-up and bad suits, danced terribly and were old enough to be her grandfathers.

Her big debut as an adult in the Telugu industry was in 1978, with *Padaharella Vayasu*—a remake of the Tamil film *16 Vayathinile,* directed by K. Raghavendra Rao. It starred Chandra Mohan and Mohan Babu. In *Badi Panthulu* (1972), she played NTR's granddaughter and later went on to play his romantic lead in *Vetagadu* (1979), *Aatagadu* (1980), *Sardar Papa Rayudu* (1980), *Kondaveeti Simham* (1981), *Bobbili Puli* (1982), *Anuraga Devata* (1982) and *Justice Chowdary* (1982). This says less about NTR's youthfulness and more about the state of the Telugu film industry at the time.

Sridevi's other notable Telugu films include *Karthika Deepam* (1979) starring Sobhan Babu, *Aakali Rajyam* in 1981 with Kamal Hassan, *Trisulam* (1983) and *Oka Radha Iddaru Krishnulu* in 1986.

She starred opposite three generations of Telugu actors: starting with NTR and ANR and moving onto Krishna, Nagarjuna, Venkatesh and Chiranjeevi. She starred with ANR in *Premabhishekam* (her magnum opus) and later with his son, Akkineni Nagarjuna, in *Govinda Govinda.* This was simply normal for Sridevi by now. She had acted as a child with Krishna and was later cast as his heroine.

In *Jagadeka Veerudu Athiloka Sundari,* which is a supernatural fantasy, Sridevi plays an angel from heaven desperately trying to be taken seriously and often slapped by her co-star Chiranjeevi. This K. Raghavendra Rao film was a blockbuster and was subsequently dubbed in Tamil as *Kadhal Devathai,* in Hindi as *Aadmi aur Apsara,* and in Malayalam as *Hai Sundhari.* Sridevi was ringing the cash registers and anything she touched was turning to gold. In fact, '*Dhak dhak*', Madhuri's evergreen track from *Beta,* was an adaptation of '*Abbani tiyyani*' by Ilaiyaraaja from the same film, with Sridevi and Chiranjeevi doing pelvic and chest thrusts in a garden.

Every Telugu movie buff will remember Sridevi's delightful performance in Ram Gopal Varma's *Kshana Kshanam* (1991), a classic masala meets western-style road movie in which she plays a goofy girl who works in an office (reminiscent of Seema in *Mr India*) and, through a series of coincidences, ends up in gangster hell with Venkatesh and Paresh Rawal (the baddie). Even as a damsel in distress, she breathed the same kind of conviction and nuance into her role in this oft-repeated trope of hero and heroine on the run from the bad guys. She won a Filmfare Award for Best Actress for this film and it is probably one of her finest performances in Telugu cinema. It's vintage Sridevi all the way—her expressions filling every frame and making an absolutely charming watch. Ram Gopal Varma declared that he wrote *Kshana Kshanam* hoping desperately that Sridevi would like it and agree to act in it. An ardent fan of Sridevi, Varma gave us a truly memorable film that is hard to tire of.

However, Sridevi was fully ensconced in Bollywood by that time. Post the stupendous success of *Himmatwala,* which was a remake of the Telugu *Ooruki Monagadu,* Telugu producers saw huge potential in Bollywood remakes with Sridevi lending her Midas touch to them. And she did. So *Trishulam* became *Naya Kadam, Devata* became *Tohfa, Chuttalunnaru Jagratha* became *Mawaali, Adavi Simhalu* became *Jaani Dost*, *Balidanam* became *Balidaan* and *Justice Chowdary* remained *Justice Chaudhury* (but NTR became Jeetendra, thankfully). They continued to back Sridevi's Hindi movies like *Chandni, ChaalBaaz, Inquilaab, Aulad* and even *Lamhe.*

In effect, Bollywood did not steal Sridevi from the south. It was Telugu producers who sold her to Bollywood. Almost all of Jeetu-Sridevi movies were remakes of Telugu movies in Hindi.

This, I had a hard time convincing Amma of.

Although Sridevi gained her pan-India stardom by moving to Bollywood, she often stated in her interviews that she missed the Telugu and Tamil industries where she felt at home. Long after she had left the south, her spot remained vacant. Nobody could fill even half her shoes—in the skills of dancing, comedy or acting. Or just finding sheer joy in the act of performance.

6

Dance Like the World Is Watching

Main khwabon ki shehzadi
Main hun har dil pe chaayiii
Badal hai meri zulfein
Bijli meri angdaaayeee
Bilji girane main hun aayyeeee
Oho bijli girane main hun aayyyeee
Kehte hain mujhko Hawa Hawaaii!

(I am the princess of dreams
I have touched many a heart
My hair is like clouds
My limbs move like lightning
Come let my lightning strike you
They call me Hawa Hawaii)

—Lyrics from *Mr India,* 1985

ON 25 FEBRUARY 1983, *Himmatwala* released and the entire Bombay film industry sat up and took notice of a voluptuous *apsara* sashaying among pots, pans and feather dusters, lip-syncing to '*Naino mein sapna*'. In this quasi-classical dance sequence, replete with glittery costumes, jewellery and props, Sridevi matches steps with her male co-star Jeetendra, then known as 'Jumping Jack'. In another song from the same film, '*Taki o taki*', Sridevi and Jeetendra are totally in sync—their movements, gestures and expressions creating a new vocabulary for a Bollywood dance sequence. She was grace in motion. *Himmatwala* was among the ten highest grossing films of the 1980s and led to Sridevi's meteoric rise in Bollywood almost overnight. But it was in her dance that she displayed the best of her versatility and control as a performer.

In May 2018, *Ladies Finger*, one of India's leading feminist webzines, hosted a Sridevi-special edition of their 'Leddis Nights' as a tribute to their favourite star. An all-women audience of five hundred in various Sridevi costumes, and an all-women line-up of stand-up comediennes, theatre and dance performers (including Aditi Mittal performing part of her new set), a female DJ, bartender, wait staff, and even a female bouncer gathered together to celebrate Sridevi. The result was a glorious night of laughter, comedy, song, dance and Sridevi-themed cocktails. It was a true reflection of the impact that Sridevi has had as a performer, as a comedic genius, as someone who took her work very seriously, but not herself. The evening was resplendent with Chandnis, Benazirs, Anjus, Manjus and, of course, Hawa Hawais. It was an awiwiwiwiwiwi kind of feeling.

In the 2017 comedy drama *Tumhari Sulu*, Vidya Balan plays Sulu, a bored but enterprising homemaker who is constantly mimicking Sridevi, Hema Malini and Madhuri Dixit and even does a full rendition of '*Batata vada*', S.P. Balasubrahmanyam-style, with her husband in bed. She soon wins a contest and turns night-time RJ who talks huskily to strangers about love. When Sulu meets with unprecedented success and they need a soundtrack to celebrate, it is Sridevi's '*Hawa Hawai*' that is the chosen one.

There is a reason Sridevi's song-and-dance sequences are etched in our visual memory.

As an adolescent, Karan Johar, a huge, crazy Sridevi fan, by his own admission to Poonam Saxena (when she was writing his biography, *An Unsuitable Boy*), used to invite his friends over and dance to '*tathaiyya tathaiyya*' (in the song '*Nainon mein sapna*') over and over again. 'I danced to "*Hawa Hawai*" when I was in school ... I have seen every film of hers multiple times ... I met her with shaking hands and feet on the sets of my father's film *Gumrah* ... and felt I had arrived when she called me for the first time ... every time I met her I had a star struck moment and a fan boy vibe ... I don't think I can believe it ... perhaps I don't think I want to believe that she is no more ... she is a huge reason I love the movies ... I feel like Indian cinema just lost its smile ...' he posted on Instagram the day Sridevi's death was announced.'[1]

In *Chandni*, we fall in love with her at first sight as we watch her frolic delightfully in the hugely popular wedding number '*Mere haathon mein*', a dance sequence that has remained an all-time favourite at Indian weddings. With her radiant *Chandni* look,

1. https://www.instagram.com/p/BfnWIa2gt6-/?hl=en

Sridevi created a new glamour code for the '80s, with endless replicas of it emerging in later years. The highlight is a three-minute-long signature classical dance sequence, where she is picturised almost as an ethereal, mythical goddess (the apsara returns) draped in white, as her lover Rohit (Rishi Kapoor), paralysed and bound to a wheelchair, remembers his happier days with her. It gave me goosebumps. She danced with such aplomb and grace that even a leading classical dancer couldn't have matched her.

In *Lamhe* Sri does the *tandav,* an angry one. When humiliated by Virendra Pratap Singh (Anil Kapoor), Pooja (Sridevi) vents her anger in a bizarre rage dance, a new-age tandav. Chinni Prakash, who choreographed '*Main aisi cheez nahin*' with Sridevi and Amitabh Bachchan in *Khuda Gawah,* said in an interview, 'When you see a dance, the first thing you see is the face. And Sridevi is excellent in the face. She is a very reactive dancer. She has a range of expressions and can react in ten different ways to a movement.'[2]

In *Jaag Utha Insaan* (1984), she does her famous temple dance and, later, a tandav dance sequence amidst *diyas.* It is, however, '*Tarpat beete tum bin ye raina*' with Mithun playing the flute that forms the heart of the story of a Brahmin girl, who is a temple dancer, falling in love with a Harijan boy. If we'd used song-and-dance sequences to take a quick loo break, Sridevi made sure you were glued to the edge of your seat. She was choreographed by the master of dancers, Gopi Krishna, in this one, and the effect shows.

In *Janbaaz* (1986), she made a sensuous and surreal guest appearance as a star singer in a red chiffon sari, belting out,

---

2. http://asridevi.blogspot.com/2011/07/sridevis-top-ten-dances.html

Jaag Utha Insan, 1984

'*Har kisi ko nahi milta yahan pyar zindagi mein*' ('Few people find love in their lifetime') against a backdrop of the ocean and endless sky. Her larger-than-life presence is spellbinding.

In *Lamhe*, when she dances along with Ila Arun to the folk tunes of '*Chudiyan khanak gayeen*' on the sandy dunes of Rajasthan, she is equally captivating in her blue-and-yellow ghagra choli and her royal demeanour. (Sridevi won the Filmfare Award for Best Actress in 1992 for her role as Pallavi (mother) and Pooja (daughter) in the film.)

Though the greatest Sridevi act was in a film that few might have seen. It's called *Naaka Bandi* and the song (get this!) proclaims, *'Main lagti hun Sridevi'*, in which she displays an entire wardrobe of talents—spoofing Mumtaz, Zeenat Aman, Madhubala, Vyjayanthimala, Rekha, Hema Malini, Meena Kumari, Asha Parekh, Rakhee, Mala Sinha, Waheeda Rehman, and does a Gabbar act in the end.

Even in the utterly OTT *Roop Ki Rani Choron Ka Raja* (1993), which was the ten-crore debacle of the decade, Sridevi tried to save the day with her dancing. In the film, she is an intrepid and funny thief and self-proclaimed 'queen of beauty' in 'the fashion and modelling world', when all we see her do is dance and sing in costumes that make *Mr India* look insipid in comparison. She couldn't save the movie, but her dancing inspired Amitabh Bachchan to send her a truckload of flowers.

She even tried something hawa-hawaish in the song '*Main roop ki rani*', complete with costume changes: red and gold dress, feather duster hat seguing into blue metallic dress and, finally, a silver outfit with rhinestone-studded hat and a cross-eyed moment. The silver dress was reminiscent of her gold dress in '*Hawa Hawai*' and Sridevi was as much into the song as ever—it's just that the song didn't deserve her. Needless to say, she made us believe she had a blast.

When I interviewed Saroj Khan for this book,[3] she told me that she still remembers when she was asked to watch *Himmatwala* by her cameraman friend Akbar, 'I wish I had such girls to work with,' was her main thought as she watched Sridevi fill the screen with her moves and her radiance. Her wish was soon granted because Subhash Ghai asked her to choreograph Sri in his next movie, *Karma* (1986), co-starring Jackie Shroff, Anil Kapoor, Naseeruddin Shah, Dilip Kumar and Nutan. In the following years, Saroj Khan and Sridevi would go on to create some of the most memorable chartbusters in over twenty-two films.

Sridevi's dancing style at the time was still characteristic of the 'Madras Masters', and some bollywoodification was necessary, thought Saroj. The *Karma* shoot was in Kashmir and incidentally Madhuri Dixit, a Saroj Khan protégée, also shot a song for the film, which Ghai decided to shelve as he felt she was too good a performer to be wasted on a cameo appearance. (He went on to cast her in *Uttar Dakshin,* which was her first big film after *Abodh,* although N. Chandra's *Tezaab* was her big hit in 1988.)

Saroj and Sridevi's relationship did not start very well. The first time they worked together was on the song '*Maine rab se tujhe*' in *Karma,* when there were thirteen retakes. When the shot was finally okayed, Sridevi came up to her and said, 'Masterji, if you think I am a great dancer, you are mistaken. I need rehearsals. Will you please give me rehearsals?' So Saroj

---

3. Interview in March 2018

Khan asked Subhash Ghai for rehearsals, and he laughed. But Sridevi and she worked it out and became friends. 'We used to do at least two songs a month, sometimes more. She told producers she wanted to work with me. In fact, she didn't give dates till she knew I was free. She always fought for me,' said Saroj.

The song '*Hawa Hawai*' in Shekhar Kapur's science fiction adventure cemented the relationship between the dancer and her guru. That song was perhaps the most spectacular side effect of a cross connection on a landline (remember those things?). Seema (Sridevi) is a goofy journalist who is constantly mistaking identities and interviewing the wrong people and struggling to find some quiet time to write. She overhears a conversation on a cross connection on the telephone which alerts her to the arrival of a certain Mr Wolcott (Bob Cristo) and puts her on the trail of a gang of smugglers. To gain entry into the smugglers' den, she goes undercover as an exotic Hawaiian dancer, (naturally called Hawa Hawai), making a grand entrance, wearing apples and grapes in her hair. She requests a room for her 'costume changes' and gets to work. In the next frame, which begins with a close up of her derriere in a shimmering gold dress, she starts to sing in a nonsense 'foreign' language, made up of the names of faraway cities of the world (of course Honolulu features prominently), then segues full on into Hindi, while trying to uncover Wolcott's secrets—thereby creating the greatest chartbuster of the '80s.

Saroj Khan's animated choreography, Laxmikant-Pyarelal's upbeat tune and Javed Akhtar's wacky lyrics were a prize cocktail. Sridevi, of course, added a lot of her own style—her trademark trick-stumbles, eye rolls, a cross-eyed moment halfway through the song. Such was her energy while shooting the song that director Shekhar Kapur wasn't sure where to place the camera; if he focused on her face, he felt he would lose out on her toes. When she danced, she danced with her whole body—so much so that Kapur felt even her toes were emoting. 'Her mind doesn't know what her body is doing,' Kapur had said.[4]

It seems that Sridevi would design her entire look for every song; each and every thing about her get-up from top to toe, including her make-up. She would call Saroj Khan to the make-up room and say, 'Masterji, look! I am dressed like this. Is it good for your song?' If Khan didn't approve, she would change everything. For '*Hawa Hawai*' she transitions from an all-gold ensemble (complete with headdress) at the start of the song to an off-shoulder white and gold outfit to the final black, white and red number in which she eventually gets caught and is chained up in the villain's den.

Only Shekhar Kapur could have had the ingenious idea of rendering the background dancers black-faced in '*Hawa Hawai*'. Because that triumphant moment was hers and hers alone; the obliteration of any distraction, human or otherwise, was necessary. '*Hawa Hawai*' in that sense is the quintessential Hindi film song at its best; it is woven into the story and also works as a standalone number.

During the *Mr India* shoot, there was no rehearsal hall, and in the manner of someone who always does her homework, Sridevi said to Saroj Khan, 'I am willing to dance in the corridor.' And that's where '*Hawa Hawai*' was rehearsed.

4. *Stardust*, April 1988

Choreographer Ahmed Khan, who was also one of the child actors in the film, remembers being called to the 'doctor's' cabin during the hospital sequence in the film.

> Sridevi was reserved at the start, but later very friendly with all the child stars in the film and she was so loving. We would have dance competitions on set and play games; she wanted to be part of our gang. Once, she called us in and asked us to teach her a few breakdance steps for the '*Hawa Hawai*' song. She was aware that I knew that form of dance and wanted to do something different in the song to bring in more variety. I told her that learning breakdance won't be easy and that it will take a lot of time but she learnt it in fifteen minutes. And then she told us, 'I am going to spoil it now.' She added comedy to it.[5]

As the song begins, she improvises to keep up with the Hawa Hawai persona. You believe her when she says, '*Bijli giraane main hoon aayee*'. That is the effect Sridevi had on your heart: she struck lightning into it. It is difficult for me to watch this song sitting still even today, over thirty years after I first watched it. When she moves, you want to burst into dance too.

At the time, Sridevi's command over Hindi was still being post-mortemed in every film, but the songs—she could make them her own. When Lata Mangeshkar or Kavita Krishnamurthy sang for her, she could lip-sync to their voices and was free to put everything into her performance—to dance, to pose, to move, to emote.

---

5. https://www.youtube.com/watch?v=KUhtfqxoxfg

Perhaps her ebullient, effervescent style and quirky, often outrageous costumes, were part of what made the songs she appeared in so memorable. Sridevi's lissom body, slender arms and attractiveness was exaggerated further by her carefully chosen attire. For example, her gold dress, famously seen in a close-up focusing on her rear in '*Hawa Hawai*', or the blue chiffon sari in which she shimmies erotically in '*Kaate nahin katte*', both from *Mr India*. In the latter, Sridevi is seen celebrating her sexuality in six yards, and undoubtedly leaving it etched in our memory as one of the most sensuous Bollywood songs ever filmed. In '*Mitwa*', from Yash Chopra's *Chandni* (1989), she holds up the pallu of her yellow lace sari and sways, tilting her head, as Rishi Kapoor looks on, before they dance across the fields. In that sense, every song 'n dance of Sridevi was an item number: she lifted the viewer's experience of many a film that was otherwise unwatchable with her grace, glamour and killer moves. Added to which was a generous dash of sequins, feathers, glitter, masks, transparent umbrellas, wet saris, snake dances and simply enormous headgear.

For a generation of queer people in India, Sridevi was an icon. Her electric appearances on screen, coupled with her often outlandish costumes and dance steps, set them free. Sridevi's characters were never passive, never simply black or white, and this resonated with members of the LGBT community who were coming to terms with their own identities. She was a hero, an artist and a star who unconsciously helped them deal with their problems through her depiction of people in conflict.

Those who grew up with her songs swore by her. 'When our homes were prisons and our families chains, Sridevi set us free. Her songs gave us fleeting glimpses of how the world would be if we could dance like we wanted to, and wear the clothes our hearts desired. In her often garish, kitschy performances, we saw the promise of a future where we wouldn't lie about who we were and what we liked,' journalist and queer activist Dhrubo Jyoti wrote in the *Hindustan Times* after Sridevi's death in February 2018.[6]

For Indian queer men, Sridevi provided a vocabulary which allowed them to protest and enact their deep erotic desires through dance. In *ChaalBaaz,* the demure Anju (Sridevi) suffers endless oppression, fit-inducing injections and lashes from a whip by her tormentor Tribhuvan (Anupam Kher), who is her *chachaji*. Dance is her only escape that she practises in secrecy. However, one day, at a party, Anju inadvertently breaks into a dance which intensifies into a tandav and ends with a resounding slap on the uncle's face. Though unintentional, this marks a dramatic moment of triumph against an invincible oppressor. The dance becomes an exaggerated expression of her resentment.

There was, of course, in the '80s, Dimple Kapadia and Padmini Kolhapure, who were popular among the LGBT community for the Bombino videos of their songs, but Sridevi was different. Harish Iyer, popular LGBT activist who first came to public attention in 2012 on *Satyamev Jayate,* hosted by actor Aamir Khan, is a Sridevi fan. Sridevi made a special appearance on the show to meet Iyer, who spoke about his child sexual abuse. 'Whenever we are challenged with anything in life, cinema serves as an escape mechanism. For

6. https://www.hindustantimes.com/bollywood/thank-you-sridevi-our-queer-icon/story-Oy6SST3RhHpSfrWSh9MZZM.html

me, it was so important to build this alternative reality around me, especially at a time when I was getting raped and coming home. For me, to forget all that and believe in a world where anything was possible was very important, and Sridevi made me believe in that.'

'When *Nagina*, the movie, released, I was young and impressionable. I witnessed Sridevi break into a "nagin dance" when Amrish Puri aka the "Snake Charmer" had come to disarm her. Her dance unconsciously portrayed my angst. I was mad at the world for trying to condition me. I was more than just a man. My feminine side wanted to be like her,' said Harish. When I interviewed him for this book, he told me about the fights between the 'Madhuri versus Sridevi' factions among queeristanis. Harish recalled, 'I remember I stopped talking to a few of my friends who switched sides. That time, the newer LGBT lot had developed a fondness for Madhuri. We used to have huge debates, which often resulted in throwing things at each other.'

Unlike Madhuri, who was an exponent of Kathak, or her south Indian contemporaries like Meenakshi Seshadri, Jaya Prada, Bhanupriya or Radha, Sridevi was not a trained dancer. What she had was an innate, untutored talent for dance despite never having studied it formally. Although dancing in a few songs in every film and working with a range of choreographers with different styles should be considered training enough. Her grace, rhythm and expressiveness were certainly natural attributes, and added to that was a combination of innocence, oomph and sparkle. She never went through the rigor of working with a guru in one style, which made her performances (and her, in them) unique. In a TV interview to Doordarshan in the 1980s, she had said, 'I didn't learn dancing. I didn't have a guru. In the south it's very important that every family should have a guru. But somehow, miss *ho gaya*. But I love dancing and I enjoy it. That is more important, I feel.'

Her natural rhythm and her face, which conveyed a million expressions, was what made her pure magic on screen. The audience couldn't wait to get to the part where Sridevi cut loose on screen. Only her sizzling acts were often with non-dancers like Anil Kapoor, Sunny Deol or Rajesh Khanna, but Sridevi seldom let you notice that. That aside, her dance pairing with Jaya Prada in *Majaal* and later *Maqsad* was incredible. Remember the famous number with the two ladies in monochrome saris, matching energies and twirls in a temple, doing a tandav of sorts, as the men, Rajesh Khanna and Jeetendra, beckon the snake god? (Thankfully, they do not dance while doing so.)

'Dance is needed for acting and acting is a part of dance. So they are both important. Sometimes, even when you don't get the right step in a dance, you can cover up with expressions, and make it look like you are really enjoying the dance ...' said Sridevi in the same Doordarshan interview.[7] Even Rekha had said that she was spellbound by Sridevi's dancing skills. 'She was a much better dancer than I was. I just managed to look like a dancer without being one.'[8]

Sridevi's repertoire was vast. Need someone to do a breakdance Michael Jackson style? Sridevi was your girl. Want

---

7. https://www.youtube.com/watch?v=LT4ZcliKezs

8. http://www.bollywoodhungama.com/news/features/rekhas-deep-connection-sridevi/

a seduction in a chiffon sari (with or without lenses)? Sridevi could wing it. Want her to sway in the Alps? Dance on a terrace in a while salwar kameez? A temple dance? Snake dance? Wedding *sangeet*? Tandav? She had it all covered.

However sexy the lyrics or innuendo-filled, Sridevi's performance never bordered on the cheap or the vulgar.

> *Meri darzi se aaj meri jung ho gayi, kal choli silayi aaj tung ho gayi (Chandni)*
>
> (My tailor and I had an argument—he stitched my blouse yesterday and it is tight today)

Even as she danced to lyrics like these, there was an earnestness about her that came in the way of her being objectified by the viewer. In *Himmatwala,* despite her conical bra tops, there is not a hint of vulgarity. Even her most erotic dances appeared tasteful. Her snake dance in '*Main teri dushman*' in *Nagina,* which mixed anger with eroticism, could have easily gone wrong and she could have become a laughing stock. In this otherwise mediocre film, full of jantar-mantars, where snakes are constantly morphing into people and vice-versa, Sridevi keeps the audiences riveted in the climactic song. As the snake charmer Amrish Puri's flute starts echoing through the walls of the haunted haveli, Sridevi, our own *ichhadaari nagin,* starts writhing to the music—combining several dance forms into one, immersing herself totally in the song. The result is a dance that is infused with a rare blend of sensuality and rage; and perhaps *Nagina* earned its place as a fantasy thriller through the sheer power of this one song.

❀

Ace choreographer Prabhu Deva, often termed as India's answer to the King of Pop, Michael Jackson, teamed up with Sridevi for the first time at the IIFA awards in 2013, matching his rubber steps to some of the hit numbers of the actress, right from *Chalbaaz* to her comeback movie *English Vinglish*. 'I am no one to judge Sridevi's dance. She has a different level of dance. It's great that I will be sharing that space with the actress.' Prabhudeva had told PTI.[9]

Saroj Khan told me that there was more dedication than talent in Sridevi when it came to dancing. 'Nothing like her dedication. Madhuri is a great dancer, but Sridevi was always more dedicated to her craft. She did the raincoat song in *ChaalBaaz* with 102 fever. Her eyes were red, but she didn't stop dancing. While shooting for *Lamhe*, her father died, so she had to fly back from London. But she returned to finish her tandav dance.'

The difference between Sridevi's dancing and any others' was that she always added her own spin to it. 'She worked really hard. She owned the song. When Sridevi was on screen, she filled it up; she was so larger than life. Her songs were like giant compositions,' says Saroj. She had a certain subtlety of movement, a softness in the bend of her bones, and especially the flick of her wrists and waist (popularly known as *lachak* in Hindi) which is hard to find even among well-trained classical dancers. We see a lot of this in *Chandni* and *Lamhe*. Directors could see her facial expressions even without cutting to a close-up, because Sridevi performed with her whole being, whether she was acting or dancing.

---

9. http://indianexpress.com/article/entertainment/bollywood/i-am-no-one-to-judge-sridevis-dancing-skills-prabhudeva/

'Sridevi looked different in every song, right from her hair to her eyes to her make-up to her accessories. She owned the look and people never forgot it. Madhuri had the same look from head to chest: wind-blown hair, make-up and a permanent smile she killed people with. Madhuri could do sexy very well, but Sridevi had such a range of expressions—naughty, funny, sober, intense, sexy. Her commitment was admirable. So much dedication she had to dance. She would keep coaxing me to do "one more retake",' says the favourite Masterji.

Much has been said about the Sridevi-Saroj Khan fallout post the rise of Madhuri Dixit in '*Ek do teen*' in *Tezaab*. In her version of the story, Saroj Khan says, 'Sridevi and I worked together for six years and numerous films continuously. One day, she called me to choreograph for a Telugu film with Chiranjeevi. She wanted a sexy song in the open air. I told her it wouldn't work. The mood wasn't right, and for a sexy song, the lighting had to be different. It had to be intimate, it couldn't be outdoors.'

Soon after, she choreographed Madhuri Dixit for '*Dhak dhak*' in *Beta,* which was inspired by the same Telugu song '*Abbanee teeyani*'. When Sridevi saw the song on screen, she was naturally miffed. More so because Sridevi had just refused *Beta* because she felt she had done too many films with Anil Kapoor. (The song looks heavily inspired by *Mr India's* '*I love you*', including the lighting and the haystack.)

This was followed by another misunderstanding during the making of *Chaand ka Tukda*. 'I had to choreograph a really bad bhangra song and it wasn't working. Salman Khan wasn't a good dancer, so the combination wasn't working. I told her so,' Saroj Khan revealed. Sridevi was hurt. 'Masterji, I think you are fed up of my face. I'm not getting good movements from you anymore. But how nicely you are giving Madhuri movements!' Masterji explained to her. 'Madhuri is getting good songs and you are not getting good songs. Madhuri's sun is going up and your sun is going down. Don't blame me.'

They decided not to work together for a year. 'Give me one hit number, and I'll say sorry. If not, you say sorry,' Saroj Khan proposed.

No song came up. They didn't speak.

A year later, Anil Kapoor showed Sridevi a song from *Rajkumar* that Saroj-ji had done with Madhuri in a pool. 'Please ask Mai to come and meet me,' she said to Anil Kapoor. They met and cried together and made up. Then they went on to do *Kaun Sachcha Kaun Jhootha* and *Judaai,* before Sridevi took her long break. They could never work together again.

7

Hero No. 1

THERE'S A SCENE in *ChaalBaaz* (1989) in which Suraj (Sunny Deol) asks Manju (Sridevi) as she is leaving a bar where they have spent quite some time guzzling beer. '*Tumhara naam kya hai?*' (What's your name?)

To which she replies, amid hiccups:

'*Suzie, Sunita ya Salma, naam se kya farak padta hai? Main toh sirf ek aurat hun jo … mardon ki banai hui duniya mein apni sha … sha … sha …*' (She's too drunk to remember the word.)

At which Sunny Deol prompts '*shart*' (terms, conditions).

'*… shart se jeena chahti hun,*' she finishes.

'Suzie, Sunita or Salma … what difference does it make? I am only a woman who is trying to live in a man's world on her own terms.'

This wasn't far from what Sridevi was (unknowingly) trying to do in Bollywood.

Cut to the '80s—a period in Hindi cinema we still look upon with disdain. The Hindi film industry was going through a low and there was no real contender for the no.1

hero position, even less so for a heroine. People were tired of Amitabh Bachchan's angry young man persona and his films were not doing well, except for the Mukul Anand films that came much later: *Hum* (1991) and *Khuda Gawah* (1992). Music had died. The angry man and his stunt-based films had largely killed music.

Sridevi couldn't have chosen a better moment to enter Hindi films.

When I spoke to Rauf Ahmed, former editor of *Filmfare*, he said, 'The arrival of Sridevi coincided with the fading of Amitabh Bachchan in a strange way. His films were not doing well. He was desperate and doing all kinds of things. After the *Coolie* accident and his long absence, people were scared to cast him.'[1]

Jerry Pinto further validates this theory: 'I have the feeling sometimes that Sridevi benefited a great deal from coming into Hindi cinema at a time when it was in one of its all-time troughs. Does anyone remember the 1980s with anything other than a feeling of mild horror? Hindi cinema was frantic for a breath of fresh air. The old formulae were no longer working. Amitabh Bachchan was in the cul de sac of middle age. He had outgrown the women he'd romanced so brutally and so successfully in the 1970s—Zeenat Aman, Rekha, Raakhee and Parveen Babi.'[2]

Since the late '70s, there were forays from the south into Bollywood, and remakes, especially of successful Telugu films, with *Lok Parlok* (1979), *Sargam* (1979) and *Takkar* (1980), which were all big hits. Jaya Prada, who starred in all three

1. Interview in March 2018
2. Interview in April 2018

and won accolades for her mute girl debut in K. Vishwanath's *Sargam,* was then 'the-girl-from-the-south-poised-to take-over-Hindi-films', in the tradition of other heroines from south India like Vyjayanthimala, Waheeda Rehman, Padmini, Hema Malini and Rekha.

Sridevi entered this scene as a part of the south package—initially with the unspectacular *Solva Sawan* (1978), which sank without a trace and, later, with *Himmatwala* (1983) and its dozen siblings. Movies that had numerous songs and dances, bizarre costumes, ridiculous storylines and slapstick dialogues. All written by Kader Khan, who was always part of the ensemble cast, either as Kuber urf Kobra or some such, along with Shakti Kapoor (his goofy counterpart).

Music was back, and Jeetendra could be 'Jumping Jack' again, and he was looking for heroines to jump with. He had already started the culture of mentoring his heroines—first with Hema Malini, with whom he did several films in the '70s and almost married (but angry Dharam paji literally lifted her off the wedding pandal). Hema was followed by Jaya Prada, whom he did twenty-four films with, of which eighteen were hits, and then Sridevi, whom he brought along from the south with *Himmatwala.* Although Jaya Prada had done the Telugu version and was miffed at this decision. The legend goes that the producers, Padmalaya Film Studios, and Jeetendra opted for Sridevi as she had more oomph and was a novelty in Hindi films as well as already being a superstar in the south.

Himmatwala, apart from being a thunderous hit and the biggest blockbuster of 1983, also earned Sridevi the moniker of 'thunder thighs', thanks to her whip-cracking scenes in leather leotards, not to mention her purple swimsuit in which she chases the flute-playing mute boy (Arun Govil), grabs his flute and throws it into the river as her girl gang cheers. However, the success of *Himmatwala* also got her a dozen more films at the price she commanded.

'Jeetu is my lucky mascot,' Sridevi would say in an interview to *Stardust*. 'I'll never forget what he has done for me. He gave me all the moral support and confidence I needed. Before he came along, I was a nobody in Hindi films.'[3]

By 1983, Telugu remakes had flooded the Hindi film industry, and *Jaani Dost* by K. Raghavendra Rao (featuring Dharmendra, Jeetendra and Parveen Babi) was among these. Interestingly, Sridevi's name didn't feature in the film's publicity posters although it was released soon after *Himmatwala*. As Karate Rani Shalu, she wore some more leather leotards and boots and kicked ass.

Sridevi worked her way into *Jaag Utha Insan* (1984), as she wanted to work with K. Vishwanath who had a penchant for casting Jaya Prada (*Sargam, Kaamchor*). She convinced Rakesh Roshan, who was producing the film, that the role was meant for her and her alone and she finally got it. Sridevi was exemplary in the movie—the story of a Brahmin girl falling in love with a Harijan boy. Her temple dances, choreographed by Gopi Krishna, were spectacular, but the movie failed at the box office because there was too much melodrama, too many good versus bad speeches and everyone died in the end.

The Sridevi-Mithun pairing had great chemistry and almost inevitably they fell in love. They were even said to have had a secret marriage. However, the *jodi* was short-lived as Sridevi's mother imposed a ban on all films with Mithun. He was also

---

3. *Stardust,* June 1983

a possessive lover who laid down conditions on what she could and couldn't wear and this didn't go down well with producers.

Then they couldn't be cast together because news of their 'secret marriage' had got out and Mithun was married to Yogeeta Bali. (Sridevi and Mithun both denied the alleged marriage.) Sridevi probably realised she didn't want to make the same mistake as Jaya Prada who had committed professional hara-kiri through a very public relationship followed by a 'secret marriage' in 1986 with producer Srikant Nahata, also a married man with children. (It ended her career in films abruptly and then she took to politics and joined the Telugu Desam Party.) Jaya Prada's exit consolidated Sridevi's position even further. The rest was a cakewalk.

Himmatwala's success made Jeetendra greedy about this gold mine he had unearthed. To make his position stronger in the south, he took the *Himmatwala* formula a little too seriously and got Sridevi to sign a spate of southern remakes, all clones of each other: *Mawaali, Akalmand, Dharam Adhikari, Balidaan, Sarfarosh, Suhaagan, Aag aur Shola, Ghar Sansar, Majaal, Justice Chaudhury, Aulad, Maqsad, Himmat aur Mehanat, Jaani Dost, Tohfa* and the gang—all remakes of Telugu or Kannada movies. Sridevi essentially gave Jeetendra's career a second innings of sorts, and he reciprocated by dancing with pots and pans. Of the nineteen films they did together, thirteen were hits.

'My onscreen pairing with Sridevi became a hit only because of her. In fact, whichever actor or film she worked with/in, became a super hit. That was her aura. She was always the real superstar,' Jeetendra said in an interview to NDTV after her death.[4]

Jeetendra had nothing to complain about, but Sri was restless. She was in her early twenties and had a long career ahead of her—she felt stuck in the kind of movies she was doing. After a few remakes, Sridevi wanted to experiment with more directors. However, since she was caught in a casting trap with Jeetendra, she was stuck with filmmakers like Dasari Narayan Rao, T. Rama Rao, K. Raghavendra Rao and K. Bapaiah. Producers and directors who signed on Jeetendra now wanted Sridevi as a package deal. Often they wanted Jaya Prada too. At one time in the mid-'80s, casting the Sridevi-Jeetendra-Jaya Prada ensemble in films became a staple. They did nine films together.

Language was a problem for both actresses: neither spoke Hindi nor cared to learn it, and it was hard to decide who sounded worse. Sridevi managed to camouflage her lack of language skills with her girly, sing-song voice and Jaya Prada, with her pristine beauty. Luckily, getting Naaz, the dubbing artist, to imitate her pitch and sing-songness solved Sridevi's language problems for the time being.

Everybody thought that maybe Jaya Prada was going to be 'No. 1' because she had the more Indian face. But directors said it was Sridevi because she had the glamour. She projected a unique combination of spunk and spark. However, Sri needed heroes other than Jeetendra to fully grow as a heroine. Her pairing with Kamal Haasan and Rajinikanth, which had worked magic in the south, wasn't exactly hit-worthy in Hindi cinema (*Sadma* was a flop, and *ChaalBaaz* was totally Sridevi's movie and the men didn't really matter).

---

4. NDTV interview on 27 February 2018

ChaalBaaz, 1989

Nagina (1986) was the turning point. Termed as the fluke hit of the decade, it was the biggest blockbuster of 1986 and proved that Sridevi could carry a film single-handedly on her shoulders. She was a crowd puller on her own. This was something no other heroine could do in the '80s. After the success of this film, producers were lining up outside her house, and her price went up even further. In fact, *Nagina* did more for her career in Hindi films than *Himmatwala* did.

Then just when you thought she was on top of her game, she changed her game.

After *Nagina,* she showcased a different kind of acting altogether in *Mr India* (1987). In it Sridevi found the range and versatility and freshness she had been thirsting for. She was an actor, dancer, performer, a hero, an all-round entertainer in the movie. It was as if Shekhar Kapur had actually picked out her best and given it a sheen all his own. To which Sridevi had added flair, all her own. *Mr India* was perhaps the most iconic role of Sridevi's career and elevated her to 'India's first female superstar' status. In the film she switches from glam doll to girl next door and dances like there's no tomorrow.

She had reached unimaginable heights. If a movie had to be a hit, it had to have Sridevi. Such was her stature that she was soon called the 'female Bachchan of Bollywood'. She was one of the only women who could headline a film without a male co-star, something incredibly rare in Indian cinema. It was like old times again, when heroines like Suraiya and Nargis had author-backed roles and dominated the scene.

Shekhar Kapur said in *Filmfare*'s August 1990 issue, 'I never miss a Sridevi film. I've seen most of her Tamil and Telugu films. I was very impressed by her performance in *Moondram Pirai*. She was brilliant ... As an actress she's remarkable. By far the most complete performer we ever had. You may call her an extension of Geeta Bali. She has surpassed Vyjayanthimala and Mumtaz. She has the passion of Meena Kumari and Nargis and the vulnerable charm of Madhubala. All she needs is to do a film like *Mughal e Azam*.'

Perhaps after all those 'angry young man' films of the 1970s, audiences were ready to see a heroine crack the whip, avenge her oppressors and take charge. They loved it when Sridevi played the central character, often with an insouciance and irreverence all her own. As Sridevi's stature grew, she veered towards roles of working women who were irreverent and left men flummoxed and often emasculated. She didn't play coy, neither did she wait for a man to rescue her; instead she took charge of her life and those of others too. She was the hero, and she retained her No. 1 position for ten enviable years. She was unique among heroines in starring in a series of solo blockbusters: *Nagina, Mr India, Chandni, ChaalBaaz* and, later, *English Vinglish*.

Sridevi charged more than any other actress of her era, and sometimes she charged as much as Amitabh Bachchan (and that's huge!). At a time when commercial Bollywood cinema was largely hero-dominated, she had the talent to command screen time on par with the heroes. Not to mention frequently overshadowing them to become the film's main draw. She was big enough for roles to be written for her: Yash Chopra made *Chandni* (1989); Shekhar Kapoor did *Mr India* (1987); Pankaj Parashar gave her *ChaalBaaz* (1989, remake of '70s hit *Seeta aur Geeta*); she did *Nagina* (1986) with Harmesh

Lamhe, 1991

Malhotra, followed by *Nigahen (Nagina Part II)*; Yash Chopra's *Lamhe* came in 1991; there was *Khuda Gawah* with Amitabh Bachchan in 1992; and *Mom* came in 2016.

From 1983 to 1990, on an average, every third Sridevi movie in Bollywood was a hit. While she was making it big in Hindi cinema, the Tamil and Telugu film industries were in mourning. Their star had been taken away by Bombay.

While Sridevi was riding high, Anil Kapoor jumped onto the bandwagon; so did Mithun Chakraborty, Sunny Deol, Rishi Kapoor, Vinod Khanna and Shatrughan Sinha. At the time, Rajesh Khanna was desperate for a second innings, so he too joined the party. He graduated from doing two-heroine films to two-hero films and Sridevi managed to keep Kaka in the game for a few more years with *Maqsad, Masterji, Nazrana* and *Naya Kadam*.

However, in an interview to *Movie* magazine in November 1987, Rajesh Khanna said, 'If you go by trade reports, she is undoubtedly the No. 1 heroine. However, ours is a male-dominated industry and a woman can never replace the hero. Never. The only heroine who posed a threat to the heroes was Hema Malini—for years. She ruled the masses and classes and the entire country came to see her. Mumtaz was also there, but she was always second to Hema.'

Sridevi then resuscitated Rishi Kapoor's career and they went on to do five films together: *Chandni, Banjaran, Nagina, Gurudev* and *Kaun Sachcha Kaun Jhootha*. Among these, *Chandni* and *Nagina* were the most successful, with the songs smashing all records.

Sridevi now called the shots; she had come a long way. 'Earlier producers used to take me for outdoor shooting to godforsaken places like Rajmundry where the shooting conditions were bad. I used to be there at their mercy for twenty days at a stretch, burning in the sun, bearing all the discomfiture. Today, it's different. My producers ask me, Madam, where would you like to shoot? Ooty, Simla, Switzerland. That's it. I guess things change with success,' she said in a *Stardust* interview in October 1989.[5]

Inquilaab, 1984

Sridevi was even able to impart a softer image on Amitabh with *Inquilaab*, *Aakhree Raasta* and *Khuda Gawah*. Producers were happy they had found a tall heroine to replace Rekha opposite the Big B (the two had stopped working together following the awkwardness of their alleged affair). However,

5. http://sridevi.biz/stardust-october-1993.html

running around in badly designed pyjama suits with smocks while Sri was in a pink shimmer dress trying to seduce him in '*Aaj abhi yahin*' (*Inquilaab*, 1984) was not very becoming of Amitabh at fifty, and, in any case, their chemistry wasn't exactly breaking the box office.

Shashi Kapoor wanted Sridevi to star in *Ajooba* along with Amitabh but she was not too keen; the role did not convince her, and it went to Dimple. Also, it was tough to put Amitabh and Sridevi in one movie because it would skyrocket the film's budget. In an interview in 1987, Sridevi said, 'I have never said I won't work with Amit-ji. But then what's there for any artist to do in a film starring him? He does everything himself.'[6]

By the time she was offered *Khuda Gawah*, Sridevi had already declared, 'No more minuscule roles in Bachchan starrers!' But she finally agreed on the condition that she would play both the roles of mother and daughter (the daughter's role was initially offered to Shaheen, Saira Banu's niece). The audience did appreciate *Khuda Gawah*, but Bachchan and Sridevi didn't have much onscreen time together since the movie was all about *viraha* (parting). The film, advertised as having India's No. 1 actor with India's No. 1 actress, was undoubtedly made on a colossal budget; it opened to a great response but was an average hit. Both Sridevi and Amitabh got rave reviews for their performances. Sridevi was nominated for best actress, and till date is the only actress who has done a double role in a movie with Bachchan. She pushed for screen time which was on par with her male co-leads, as well as for equal pay—long before these were widely discussed topics.

---

6. *Filmfare*, November 1987

In many ways Sridevi's career mirrored Bachchan's with whom she was constantly compared. They both started out as purely actors under serious filmmakers: Bachchan with K.A. Abbas and Hrishikesh Mukherjee; Sridevi with K. Balachander, P. Bharathiraja and J. Mahendran. Just as Bachchan made the transition from actor to star through Salim-Javed films and, later, as an all-round entertainer-performer with the films of Manmohan Desai and Prakash Mehra, so did Sridevi—except for her, the transition was from Tamil/Telugu to Hindi films.

The Anil Kapoor-Sridevi jodi didn't create much magic at the box office. Of their thirteen films together, only five were hits: *Judaai, Laadla, Janbaaz, Mr India* and *Karma* (and they were not always paired with each other). The rest were flops: *Roop Ki Rani Choron Ka Raja, Aasman se Gira, Heer Ranjha, Lamhe, Joshilaay, Gurudev, Mr Bechara, Sone pe Suhaaga* and *Ram Avtar.* The most beloved film was, of course, *Mr India,* in which Anil remained largely invisible. The role was originally written for Amitabh, who did not do the film because of differences with Salim-Javed and, for years, it was Anil's biggest claim to fame that he had walked into a role originally written for Mr Bachchan.

Another pairing which failed at the box office was Sridevi and Sunny Deol. They worked together in *Sultanat* (the 1986 movie which became famous as Karan Kapoor's disastrous debut), *Nigahen* (1988), *Joshilaay* (1989), *Main Tera Dushman* (1989) and *Ram Avtar* (1988)—all duds. Their only hit film together was *ChaalBaaz* (1989), but it had two Sridevis instead of one, so you can imagine what was left for the men to do. Rajinikanth still managed a memorable scene with *'Aaj Sunday hai, aaj peene ka din hai'*, but poor Sunny was left high and dry as Sridevi waltzed in the rain with her raincoat and umbrella in '*Na jaane kahan se aayi hai*', and went on to win the Filmfare Award for Best Actress for her performance. He vowed never to work with her again.

Around the same time, Sridevi also worked with Daddy Deol, Dharmendra, in *Farshitay, Naaka Bandi, Sone pe Suhaaga, Watan ke Rakhwale, Sultanat* and *Jaani Dost*. However, the two were paired with each other only in *Naaka Bandi*.

She worked with Govinda for the first time in *Gair Kanooni* (1989), a movie that had audiences whistling to her comic performances. Govinda had pleaded with film director Prayag Raj to get him the role opposite Sridevi. It became a hit at the box office and is the only Sridevi-Govinda starrer.

Sherni, 1988

By now, Sridevi was used to doing title roles (where the movie posters said: *Sridevi: In and as ...*) like *Sherni*, opposite Shatrughan Sinha, in which she does stunts in a *chaniya choli* and jumps on rooftops.

When Vinod Khanna made a comeback, post his Osho phase, Sridevi played his love interest in two out of the three films, *Pathar ke Insan*, *Farishtay* and the super hit *Chandni*.

With Jackie Shroff there was *Halla Bol* (guest appearance for both), *Roop Ki Rani Choron Ka Raja*, *Pathar ke Insan*, *Main Tera Dushman*, *Jawab Hum Denge* and *Karma*. Nothing earth-shattering happened.

In 1996, Shah Rukh Khan made a guest appearance in *Army*, an out and out Sridevi film where he was killed off quite early; the rest of the movie is dominated by Sridevi and her five-man army. SRK is known to have famously said, 'I did the film so I could tell my children I worked with an icon!'[7]

In the year 2004, *Meri Biwi ka Jawaab Nahin*, Sridevi's only film with Akshay 'Khiladi' Kumar, released in cinema halls. It had Sridevi playing a country bumpkin, Durga, who speaks only in rhymes with a Bhojpuri accent and passes time spying on people and gossiping with the *paan*-seller Gangu. Although the film was shot in 1994, the release was delayed because the producer went absconding and there was no money to complete the movie. The bizarre climax, one that seems stitched together as an afterthought, had body doubles replacing the lead pair.

In an episode of *Koffee with Karan*, Akshay Kumar spoke about this: 'Sridevi and I hold hands and we say that

---

7. *CineBlitz*, July 1996

we will take revenge in the film. But we did not shoot the revenge part. A text on the screen reads '*Un dono ne milke phir badla liya*' (They both later take their revenge), and the film ends.'[8]

By the mid-eighties, Sridevi was tired of the southern remakes and the *Himmatwala* brand of films, and became picky. This infuriated her 'makers', including K. Raghavendra Rao, T. Rama Rao and A. Poornachandra Rao (of Padmalaya Film Studios, which produced *Himmatwala*). Soon they started casting Meenakshi Seshadri and Bhanupriya in their films, but they couldn't recreate the Sridevi magic.

Sri didn't care. Once she was offered a role in a film called *Kaamyab* opposite Jeetendra, which she rejected. The producers, Padmalaya, were reportedly miffed so they signed another southern actress, Radha, in her place. Later, posters of the other actress were seen all over the city with the tagline: 'She's not Sridevi. She's Radha!' Upset by the production house's childish behaviour, Sridevi's mother asked her not to work in another film, *Hoshiyar,* which she had signed with them earlier. The film was later done by Meenakshi Seshadri.

Such was Sridevi's stature that when Feroz Khan was making *Janbaaz,* he was asked by distributors to cast Sridevi. He was reluctant to do so as he had not been impressed by her performance in *Himmatwala*. However, giving in to the distributors' advice, he decided to call her and offered her the

---

8. https://scroll.in/reel/871000/in-meri-biwi-ka-jawab-nahin-a-vigilante-sridevi-and-a-climax-that-wasnt

main role. Sridevi rejected the role as it called for baring lots of skin (the role went to Dimple). That's when the character of Seema was created. *Janbaaz* featured Sridevi in a song, '*Har kisi ko nahi milta yahan pyaar zindagi mein*', which had her lighting up the screen in a red chiffon sari.

Sridevi recalled in an interview to Subhash K. Jha in May 2009, soon after Feroz Khan's death:

> At first I was hesitant because it was just a guest appearance. Also the presentation seemed a little too sensuous for my personality. But when Mr Khan spoke to me in my mother tongue I was immediately convinced. Yes, I was as surprised as you are. But he spoke fluent Tamil ... He was a very classy gentleman and his cinema reflected that. I was very proud to be in *Janbaaz*. I'm glad people still remember me in that brief role. It's all because of Mr Feroz Khan's presentation that I made an impact in *Janbaaz*. It proved it's not about the length of the role but the impact.

When Boney Kapoor saw Sridevi sashaying sensuously against the backdrop of the ocean, he was blown away by the effect. He was producing *Mr India* then and challenged Shekhar Kapur, the director, 'Show me something like this!'

Unperturbed, Shekhar said, 'Of course!'

The result was '*I love you*'. The chiffon sari was now blue and there was rain to amp up the amorousness.

From the mid-'80s to the early '90s, Sridevi's domination of the box office was complete and total; no one could touch her. She had upstaged all her rivals effortlessly—whether it was Jaya Prada, Dimple, Rekha, Rati Agnihotri, Poonam Dhillon, Kimi Katkar or Meenakshi Seshdari. She had zoomed far ahead, where she had no competition, even from her heroes.

Actresses who were once wary of her had now come to terms with the phenomenon that was Sridevi.

'I can't describe it. *Ek zing hai,*' said Dimple to *Movie* magazine in October 1987. Amrita Singh articulated it further, 'Except for Sridevi, all the other heroines including myself can be slotted together. I'm afraid it is reality and it's time we face it. Today, most producers are proposal makers and most heroines are interchangeable. Sridevi is the only actress who makes a difference in the selling price of a film. She is there for keeps. Take it or leave it.'[9]

Once in an interview, when asked about Sridevi, Salman Khan had said, 'It's good to work with an actress like Sridevi. But I'm scared. She has the reputation of finishing off the hero with her performance.'[10] Aamir Khan told *Movie* magazine in an interview in 1990 following his famous cover shoot with Sridevi for the magazine's relaunch, 'I want to work with Sridevi and I want her to be a heroine in all my films. I would love to do a *Summer of '42* with her.'[11] He was three films old and had made a sensational debut with *Qayamat Se Qayamat Tak* (*QSQT*) in 1988.

Producers too made films to suit her tastes. Filmmaker Harmesh Malhotra once said, 'I make films for Sridevi. The co-stars are not important. If people can make films for Amitabh, why can't I make films for Sri?'[12] If heroes felt short-changed, or complained there was nothing for a man to do in a Sridevi movie, it was really their problem, not hers.

---

9. *Showtime,* January 1989
10. *Filmfare,* January 1992
11. *Movie,* April 1990
12. *Star & Style,* July 1991

Call it the Yashraj effect, but post *Chandni* (1989), Sridevi underwent a complete reinvention of herself—her sense of style was transformed, her rough edges were smoothened out, and she had trimmed down dramatically. She looked and dressed her best during this period and perhaps it had to do with her discovery of Manish Malhotra. *Chandni* was one of the biggest box office hits of 1989. The film won the National Film Award for Best Popular Film of 1989. Sridevi won the Filmfare Award for Best Actress the same year, but it was for *ChaalBaaz,* and Yash Chopra never got over it as he believed her role in *Chandni* was far superior.

Yash Chopra said of her, 'Sridevi's screen personality is sheer magic. You can never really guess what she's capable of until she switches herself on in front of the camera. You can't compare her with any heroine of the past. She's one of a kind. Yet you see in her almost every great actress of the past. She could easily stand in for any of them.'[13] She disrupted Bollywood's male supremacy on her own terms. Like, for example, as a shape-shifting *nagin,* when she danced to her snake-charmer's tunes in *Nagina,* with her green eyes killing her tormentor as she mouthed the lyrics, '*Main teri dushman, dushman tu mera*' (I am your enemy, and you mine). If you watch the song, you notice a subtle shift of power—the oppressor had suddenly become the oppressed.

Yes, she did wear outrageous outfits, over-the-top makeup, headdresses, wigs, sequins and lenses and she did dance against the backdrops of lotuses and waterfalls, pots and pans, but she

---

13. *Filmfare,* August 1990

did it all her way. She managed to infuse fun into her scenes. It was as though she was rebelling even as she was following instructions.

As her popularity grew, directors continued to put her in situations and dances that were designed to titillate, but she turned the tables on them by transforming those scenes into something she truly enjoyed. She seemed to exude confidence through every pore and performed to everyone's delight. However slinky the outfit or suggestive the choreography, all it took was an eye roll here, a drop trick there, and she had trademarked it to be all her own.

As Yash Chopra once said, 'In the star hierarchy, there are at least six vacant rungs after Sridevi. She is the only heroine who commands a sustained fan following. People come to see *her*, even if the film is not up to the mark.'[14]

In her column in the *Hindustan Times*, Poonam Saxena called her the first modern female superstar, someone who did it all on her own terms:

> What set Sridevi apart from other, earlier leading ladies in Hindi cinema was that she made a roaring success of films that revolved around her—rare in an industry dominated by heroes. It was unusual for filmmakers to write scripts centred around the heroine, and for these films to do well commercially meant that the star in question had forged a very special bond with audiences. A connection had been established, something most actors would kill for. How did Sridevi make this connection? Was it her traditional, Indian, chubby, doll-like beauty? Her electrifying dancing? Her

---

14. *Filmfare*, 1989

screen presence that combined seductiveness with steely strength? Her undeniable talent? That mobile, expressive face? Perhaps it was a combination of all this, with that inexplicable 'x' factor.[15]

15. https://www.hindustantimes.com/bollywood/sridevi-the-rough-diamond-who-transformed-into-first-modern-female-superstar/story-T9mfMqt8uaRGCCOSAkeuvI.html

8

That Thing You Do

Na jaane kahan se aayi hai
Na jaane kahan ko jayegi
Diwana kise banayegi yeh ladki!

(Don't know where's she's come from
Don't know where she is going
Don't know whose heart she'll win
This girl!)

—Lyrics from *ChaalBaaz,* 1989

IN A SCENE FROM *Mr India,* Seema (Sridevi) is chained up in a smuggler's den in full costume, soon after she poses as an exotic dancer and gets the entire gang dancing to her tunes in '*Hawa Hawai*'. Mr India makes a timely appearance and frees her of her handcuffs, taking the smugglers to task and giving them a little lecture on the *aam aadmi.* As they stand stunned and perplexed by what just happened, Seema realises this could make a good story for her newspaper (she has a day job as a crime reporter). So she quickly grabs a mini pad from a smuggler's jacket and a pen from another and begins to interview Mr India. 'So how long have you been in the invisibility profession?' she starts.

That pretty much sums up Sridevi's work ethic. No matter what the role or how ridiculous the situation, she was always trying to do her job. And do it as well as she could. Take, for instance, her role in *Gurudev* as the street-smart cookie, with a toothpick hanging out of her mouth, unabashedly doing things for pleasure (*mood banane ko,* as she explains it). Watch her in that hospital scene where she, pretending to be all cutesy, convinces the watchman as she tries to smuggle in some liquor for her boyfriend, pretending it is '*jawaani ki nishani ka pani*', with that trademark Sridevi glint in her eyes. Or that scene in *Roop Ki Rani Choron Ka Raja* where her character Seema Soni pretends to be a paan-chewing woman from Tamil Nadu with an exaggerated Hindi accent, head tilting at opportune moments.

In *Mr India,* which gave her a range like never before and established her as a female superstar, she exudes the innocence of a woman who is still a child at heart—goofy, mischievous, unaware of her appeal—and also a creature of desire. The '*I love you*' song, conceived by Shekhar Kapur and embodied by Sridevi, addressed the collective fantasy of an entire nation; it was as though she was speaking to every man individually—because she was making love to an unseen one. For generations of women who have always been groomed to mask desire, this was an erotic revolution. Javed Akhtar, who co-wrote the film, had said of Sridevi, 'She was the first heroine who had no qualms in expressing herself fully through her body.'[1]

---

1. As told to Rauf Ahmed, then *Filmfare* editor

'Filming *Mr India* songs and the Charlie Chaplin sequence with Sridevi were one of the most joyful moments of my directing experience. Her intuitive sense of the comic and the sensual are amazing,' Shekhar Kapur had said in a *Deccan Chronicle* interview.[2] Vidya Balan, a huge Sridevi fan, would take the admiration a notch higher: 'I think for an actor you have to be shameless, uninhibited and, if it's comedy, you have to raise it a few notches. This is a rarity, especially from a female actor. There is nothing Sridevi cannot do. After *Mr India,* she could have just packed her bags and people would still remember her for centuries.'[3]

In *English Vinglish,* there's a scene in which her insensitive husband declares in front of the family that his wife was born to cook. She stands there, silent, looking at him, her eyes speaking more than words could ever say. In those eyes, there was a whole masterclass in acting.

It was as though the camera was her private mirror. She wasn't shy; she lit up before it and gave it her all. She seemed to derive a special thrill from facing the camera and that transformed her entire being. Perhaps this is why the term 'switch on, switch off actress' became attached to her. Through all her roles, she unleashed a wholesome concoction of femininity, freedom and fun. Whatever Sridevi did on screen, worked. As the audience, we picked up every nuance—

---

2. https://www.deccanchronicle.com/entertainment/bollywood/131117/will-never-forget-making-of-mr-india-because-of-sridevis-brilliance-shekhar-kapur.html

3. MAMI Movie Mela, 2017, https://www.thenewsminute.com/article/rise-female-superstar-how-sridevi-delivered-early-blows-glass-ceiling-77009

whether she was making a face at someone behind their back in a 'I'm going to get you, but not right now' way, or a tiny wobble of her lower lip or a twinkle in her eye. She did it all for us.

Sadma, 1983

If the role or the movie didn't make sense, she worked even harder. Like Jeetendra said: 'You may find a fault with the film, but no one could find a fault with her performance.'[4] It is true that often her talent was met with absolute rubbish, but many were happy to consume it.

Naseeruddin Shah had once said of commercial cinema that it takes an elevated level of acting to do something that an actor doesn't believe in, when one finds it ridiculous. But

4. https://www.youtube.com/watch?v=YWYyez5FJ7c

Sridevi could take that leap. How else could anyone do all that she did? How could you be writhing like a nagina without believing in it? It's hard to be a mainstream actor if you are condescending of the work you do. That's why Sridevi was so successful. No matter how ridiculous the role, she enacted it like she believed in it.

Sridevi made no bones about the fact that she worked for name, fame and money.[5] When probed about creative satisfaction, she was honest enough to say, 'I don't want to lie. It is very difficult to relate success to creative satisfaction in the kind of films we make. You rarely get a great role to perform. The challenge lies in making crazy situations entertaining. It requires a high level of competence. I try my best to look different in every film I do and vary the way I dance and perform.'

Sridevi always seemed to be there 100 per cent for her role, however ridiculous. In fact, the less sense the role made, the more present she was. Perhaps that's why we took her seriously as she tried to pose as an undercover agent in a den full of smugglers, or made love to an invisible man. Or even when she tried to combat a snake charmer with her writhing and wriggling and with eyes that could kill. In a sense, Sridevi raised the bar in masala movies where the focus used to be on the male star; she often played the bubbly and cute fool, but the difference was that her acting added an enviable charm to the role. She quickly learned to maximise any role given to her, from the downright ridiculous to the over-the-top dramatic, always keeping the self-respect of the character and the actor

5. *Filmfare*, April 1989

intact. Making fun of yourself when you are in a crappy film is a hard thing to do. Sridevi made it look like serious work.

Yes, it's true that she did more bad films than good, but that's because more bad films get made than good ones.

Kamal Haasan, her co-star in twenty-seven films, often joked that Sridevi had a bag of tricks and every time she pulled out something new when she faced the camera.

I think acting for her was 'play' in its purest sense. It was as though she took 'play' and then set it free. So once in a while, the demure Anju in *ChaalBaaz,* who yearned to dance Bharatnatyam, would break into a tandav and unwittingly slap her tyrant of an uncle. To the audience, it all looked entirely plausible when Sri did it.

Nawazuddin Siddiqui, who was her co-star in her last film *Mom,* and who is himself a torch bearer for a different

Sadma, 1983

kind of sensibility in Hindi cinema, admits to having studied Sridevi very closely when he was training to be an actor. 'She brought nuance and depth and detail to commercial cinema in the '80s.'[6] And that is big, for an otherwise dismal period in the movies.

The thing about her was that she brought nuance to everything—whether it was making those comic faces, doing silly sequences when needed, or turning utterly stoic and dignified, or being a 'hunter-wali' spoilt rich girl in leather leotards who goes whining to her daddy because someone didn't let her pluck mangoes from their orchard. Her practised spontaneity was quite different from method acting and it's what she always relied on. 'I have never learned acting,' she once said in an interview. 'I think it has to come from inside.'[7]

It always did.

She was, by her own admission, a director's actor and she delivered on all the diverse roles they thought up for her. When she moved to Bollywood from the south, the films relied more on her glamour, her larger-than-life-ness, but she dug into her bag of tricks and gave what her directors wanted. If Feroz Khan wanted her to look unimaginably sexy, she did; if Yash Chopra wanted demure sophistication in a chiffon sari, she took it to another level; if a Shekhar Kapur wanted a Charlie Chaplinesque routine, she made you want for the scene to never end; if a Balu Mahendra wanted an ingénue, she was fully present; if Harmesh Malhotra wanted her to be

---

6. https://www.youtube.com/watch?v=f-rz90dgdsg

7. https://www.businesstoday.in/trending/entertainment/remembering-sridevi-i-am-an-ordinary-person-just-another-parents-daughter/story/271435.htm

a shape-shifting nagin, she gave him the best that ever was. Enough for him to make two more films that revolved around her (*Nigahen* and *Sherni*).

Adil Hussain, her co-star in *English Vinglish*, remembers being flummoxed by her 360-degree focus, absorbing everything around her, yet always being in the moment.

> The thing about Sridevi was that she was amazingly curious, yet silent; she had this power of grasping and a tremendous love for the art of acting. She treated the camera as the audience and bonded with it with utter truthfulness ... Her eyes didn't hide anything; they betrayed every feeling. I don't know if she did this knowingly or whether she was aware of it. May be she was not; she didn't know any other way except for being truthful. Through her vulnerability and her eyes, she expressed her innermost feelings. And the Indian audience loved that. In that sense, she brought an Indianness to her acting.[8]

Yash Chopra said, 'She went a step further. She didn't know the language; assistants told her the dialogues. But she contributed so much to each dance, scene, emotion. They all have something extra.'[9]

Perhaps acting became her being, having had the opportunity to flirt and interact with the camera from the age of four—an innings that is rare for any actor—along with a spectrum of experiences that were enhanced by the five different languages she acted in. An important component of

---

8. Interview in April 2018

9. Rachel Dwyer, *Yash Chopra: Fifty Years of Indian Cinema,* https://scroll.in/reel/819198/chandni-turned-around-yash-chopras-fortunes-but-he-initially-called-it-a-suicide-attempt

Sridevi's repertoire were her songs and her ability to elevate them with her expressions—some lasting only for few seconds, but leaving you with their impact forever. In every single popular Sridevi song, there is always something to latch on to. When she was on screen, she lit it up, all 70 mm of it. If at one time I focused on her dance movements, now I pay heed to her facial expressions. There is so much of her to take in that you can only do it by repeated viewing. Each time, you find something new.

Anupama Chopra, author, film critic and director of the MAMI film festival, summed it up beautifully when I spoke to her.

> She had a real solid screen presence—not the warm, inviting presence of a Madhuri Dixit—but something far more imposing. She was big in the little things she did with her performances, which made them memorable. When you watched her in *Khuda Gawah,* she was not a Bachchan heroine showing up for the mandatory two songs. She was an equal, a powerhouse, because she could balance the aura of a star with being such a fine actor. But there was an unsaid boundary about her that you would never cross. The kind of regality with which she held herself—you wouldn't dare do it.[10]

Sri often improvised on set and directors marvelled at her professionalism, the smoothness of her shot taking. Pankaj Parashar, who directed her in *ChaalBaaz,* says the whole drunken scene with Sunny Deol in the bar was improvised as she didn't think the original scene was funny enough. When

10. Interview in June 2018

Manju, after guzzling one too many beers prepares to leave, saying '*Achha, main ghar jaa rahi hun…*', Sooraj asks her, '*Tumhara ghar kahan hain?*' To which she replied, '*Mera ghar? Mera ghar bahut bada hai—itna bada hai, itna bada hai ki ek kamre se doosre kamre tak jaane mein bahut time lagta hain, isliye sochti hun ki ek cycle le loon …*'

It seems Sunny Deol was totally ill-prepared for the improv, and fumbled for words. But that made the scene a winner.

As much as it came intuitively to her, Sridevi never enjoyed talking about the process of acting. 'She was too sweet, too polite, to the point of being diffident in interviews even until my last one with her for *Mom*, where she let Nawazuddin and Akshay do the talking,' said Anupama Chopra.

Rajinikanth, who jokingly call her 'Srideva', said: 'In front of the camera and behind the camera, there were two Sridevis. Behind the camera she was very unassuming. She would listen to everything. In front of the camera she was like fire, an electric power would pass. That's how she would act. At the same time, she had never gotten angry on anyone. When she went to the Hindi film industry, she didn't know a word of Hindi. She surprised everyone with the ease and effortlessness with which she performed there. She was a born actor.'[11]

Sridevi often took on the onus of avenging the oppressed in many of her on-screen avatars. She had a steady record of tracking down her oppressors, either in leather pants (black mostly) or leather skirt (black, usually, with stockings and boots to match), hunter in hand. It is with this hunter that she makes an entry as Karate Rani Shalu (*Jaani Dost*), trying

11. https://www.thenewsminute.com/article/when-sridevi-spoke-about-getting-paid-more-friend-rajini-same-movie-77021

to teach a lesson to eve teasers. It's the same hunter that she unleashes on Shoma Anand in *Himmatwala.* Though that was mostly a waste of a hunter and more of a power play by a pricey Thakur girl. Once she had enough dance practice with the chaste Jeetendra, the whip and the leather leotards didn't make a further appearance.

In *ChaalBaaz,* she descends on her uncle Tribhuvan, whipping him nice and proper in the same manner that he had been whipping her twin sister for years. In her orange glitter top with pearl buttons and elaborate sleeves and orange trousers (with matching orange stilettos) and larger-than-bangle earrings, you tend to take her seriously, for she means business. Once she is done with the whip-cracking session, she is so hungry she orders a meal instantly from Daadu (Annu Kapoor). *'Mujhe bahut bhook lagi hai, Daadu,'* she says, *'jaldi se khaana do.'*

Although Mahesh Bhatt's *Gumrah* (1993) is known for Sridevi's melodramatic outburst in jail, there is a quiet moment when Anupam Kher (her missing father, but she doesn't know it yet) comes to visit her in jail to plan her escape. He hands her a pair of spectacles through the visitor's window, which she has to put on so he can take a photo for a fake passport. As she gingerly puts it on, he whispers, asking her to smile for the camera and she fakes a smile, her lips curling ever so slightly. We see this through the grill of the jail window, but because it was Sridevi, the image lasts in our head longer than it normally would.

In all this, there was no method, no training; everything was instinctive. Once, in an interview to Khalid Mohamed for *Filmfare,* she explained that she had never really assessed herself as an actress. 'I haven't. ... For an actress, there can be no beginning, no end ... I am always playing another girl, another woman. If I was ever asked to play Sridevi, the character would be very boring, no one would go to see the film. I keep to myself, I'm not talkative. But the audience always wants to see a bright and bubbly, *chulbuli ladki* on screen. I act spontaneously, maybe because no one in our rushed system of working has time for rehearsals.'[12]

She also said: '... a husband, father or brother dies and I have to cry and cry till my eyes hurt. But when my father died in real life, it was different, very different. There were no dramatics, no hysteria. Instead, there was a feeling of total shock, a numbness. I went blank in one fast stroke. In films, perhaps you have to scream to convince the audience that you're truly grief-stricken. Perhaps you can do a death scene realistically only in an art movie. But then I haven't acted in art movies.'

Gauri Shinde, who made her debut as a movie director with *English Vinglish,* when asked if it was overwhelming to work with such a huge star, said:

> She made sure it wasn't overwhelming. She was Shashi on the sets. She is such a treasure trove of talent. You keep drawing out and there's still more to be explored. She is not a method actor—she won't make sweeping claims about 'research', she will not say she visited middle-class houses to see what the housewives are like; she is just an instinctive actor. I don't know where it comes from, but she slipped into the character like it was always her. There

---

12. http://sridevi.biz/filmfare-december-1992.html

> was not that much talking and theorising, like 'What do you think Shashi (the character's name) would have done two years ago?' Given I'm so new, she placed her complete trust in me, followed what I asked her to do. She never tried to direct me, throw her opinions on me... she had a way of surrendering to her character, becoming the person she was playing![13]

In *Mom* and *English Vinglish,* there is a certain stillness to her face, a restraint in her body. In that containment, however, lay several powerful moments, as though she was saying that she wasn't done. In an interview on NDTV after *Mom,* she said that the day you feel that, you might as well stop acting. And that she still felt like it was her first movie, that she was a newcomer.[14]

From *Moondru Mudichu* to *Mom,* Sridevi portrayed women breaking barriers with their will alone, rising above all odds. Both women and men were able to identify with her roles. Perhaps therein lies the secret to her success. In a film industry that rarely give female stars the longevity that is generously offered to less talented male colleagues, Sridevi's extraordinary combination of acting, comic timing, arresting screen presence, beauty, dancing and her ease with both serious roles and flashy commercial extravaganzas gave her an iconic status that translated into box-office reliability and a pan-India fan following. Quite a feat for someone who just focused on showing up and doing her job.

---

13. https://www.firstpost.com/entertainment/gauri-shinde-on-english-vinglish-and-why-sridevi-is-a-treasure-of-talent-472160.html
14. https://www.youtube.com/watch?v=-MINMCG7KzE

9

Body Image and Other Matters

Ladki nahi hai tu lakdi ka khamba hai
Bak bak mat kar, naak tera lamba hai
Aa gaya kahan se tu bada hi nikamma hai
Ja ke chhup ja tu wahan jahan teri amma hai

[You are not really a girl, you are a bean pole
Don't you jabber too much, your nose is too long... (Boy)
Where have you come from, you good-for-nothing
Go home and hide in your mother's lap... (Girl)]

—Lyrics from *Himmatwala,* 1983

SRIDEVI WAS NOT the only actress in quest of a perfect figure or face. Perhaps her story is the story of every beautiful woman who never thinks she is 'enough'. In her early films as a heroine, she was still child-woman. Slim-waisted, yet full-figured, curves in the right places and a face that belied her femininity—innocent, vulnerable, playful and with oh so expressive eyes.

Jerry Pinto says, 'In some ways, Sridevi fit in with what the Indian man's dream woman is. She must be an innocent neck upwards but the rest of her body must suggest the sexually available woman. In a way, Sridevi pre-empted the anime cartoon which turns every woman into a schoolgirl, a promiscuous schoolgirl. Her face is that of a child, her eyes big, her chin pointed, but neck downwards, she is fully grown. This blurs the line between the acceptable and the illegal, which is perhaps one of the functions of the fantasy.'[1]

Unusually for her time, she stood tall, at five feet seven inches. One of the side effects of moving to Bollywood from Tamil and Telugu films was that she finally got to work with men her height (occasionally taller). In the south, she had to awkwardly romance men who didn't quite match up—whether it was Kamal Haasan or Rajinikanth in Tamil films or Akkineni Nageswara Rao, Chandra Mohan, Mohan Babu, Krishna or Chiranjeevi in Telugu. Later on, with Venkatesh and Nagarjuna arriving on the scene, things had improved, but not quite. It's a good thing she never learned to slouch.

Sridevi was the quintessential big girl who wore herself bigger, what with her fancy headgear, wigs, props, accessories and false eyelashes that spoke a thousand words. She was taller and broader than most actresses in the '80s (Madhuri Dixit, Jaya Prada, Juhi Chawla, Dimple Kapadia) and appeared more so because of her screen presence. In Saroj Khan's words, they were all tiny tots in front of Sridevi. But she was always under scrutiny—if it was not for her nose or her thighs, it was her full hips or screechy voice. For decades, as a film culture, we'd revered the tiny, the petite, the soft-spoken, the pint-sized and raised that image to a pedestal. Sharmila, Jaya, Saira, Tina, Juhi, Madhuri, Kajol, Rani were all perfect pocket-sized Indian

1. Email interview, March 2018

beauties for the perfectly medium-sized Kumar, Khan, Khanna or Kapoor. They could be carried, flung in the air, transferred from hip to hip, rolled on the lawn like carpet grass, and they fit into the crook of their arms like sleeping bags.

When Zeenat Aman came on the scene, she was called androgynous, like it was a bad thing. She was immediately cast into a category of her own and offered mostly 'modern woman' or 'other woman' roles. Of course, with her Miss India background and Rodeo Drive sense of fashion, she embraced it all with sweet vengeance. There was a panache in the way she wore bell bottoms or an evening gown, or even a bikini.

That's when Rekha (5'7") or Hema Malini (5'6") came in, and people wondered who were these dream girls, these apsaras with wide-set expressive eyes, high foreheads, perfect pouts and aquiline noses who were also taller and grander in their presence than the average Indian male? There was always a sexiness attached to their images that that was quite different from the petite sensuality of a Sharmila Tagore or even a Dimple. Thankfully for the apsaras, they quickly got paired with towering, brawny male actors like Amitabh Bachchan and Dharmendra in a string of hits.

In 2018, when Sonam Kapoor, Sridevi's niece by marriage, got married to her maverick designer fiancé Anand Ahuja, it was as if all of India was celebrating on social media with them. It was a moment for tall young women. At five feet nine inches, Sonam towered over him in ways that showed her ease in being svelte and tall and still very much in love with a shorter man. Ahuja, to his credit, beamed up in pride at his gorgeous wife in her custom monogrammed heels as they danced and celebrated in coordinated wedding finery. It made one wish Sridevi had been around to witness this cultural shift in the very heart of Bollywood—where her contemporaries, Salman Khan (5'7"), Shahrukh Khan (5'7"), Saif Ali Khan (5'4") and Anil Kapoor (5'7"), danced the night away celebrating the couple who had just turned the tables on what is acceptable or not for a tall Indian woman looking to get married. These were the same gentlemen who'd not so long ago stood on stools in tight close-ups and mid-shots next to actresses like Shilpa Shetty, Sushmita Sen or Tabu because how, oh how, could the audience possibly digest the man being shorter?

Sridevi wasn't quite as lucky. Her heroes usually looked like they struggled while transferring her from hip to hip. The whispers of thunder thighs, big hips, shoulders too broad soon started to make the rounds. Her pairing with Mithun worked because of their chemistry, but Amitabh Bachchan and Vinod Khanna looked like the only heroes who could match her. However, they never ended up doing many movies together.

In an interview to *CineBlitz* in 1985, Sridevi opened up about it saying, 'Although I am 5'7", I still love wearing high heels. Good height gives a woman a lot of dignity. But sometimes I can't wear heels because my heroes are not tall enough, like Kaka. Do you know in one of the *Karma* sequences I look taller than Jackie? He was barefoot and I had worn high heels.'[2]

Seeing how important it was for her to feel like she belonged, it wouldn't be a stretch to think she was probably taller than five feet seven inches but was discounting it in that interview so she could pass the low bar Bollywood had set for itself.

---

2. http://www.freepressjournal.in/entertainment/i-was-a-very-shy-and-lonely-child-sridevi/646895

In the same piece she went off into a stream of consciousness spiel about Sylvester Stallone: 'I am crazy about Sylvester Stallone. I have seen all three parts of *Rocky* innumerable times. He is the sexiest man I have ever come across. And one of the finest actors. His voice gives me goose flesh. God, even when I talk about him, I can feel something happening to me. My body tingles all over. Whenever I feel depressed I have to only see his film on video and I feel good again.'

One can't help but remember that just like Sridevi, Stallone was also that vulnerable, child-faced, tall man who didn't look like he quite knew what to do with his long limbs. He just lumbered around in every film, except the ones that made good use of all that height, clambering through jungles in Vietnam or bouncing off the rails of a boxing ring.

Bollywood did Sridevi no such favours. Roles suited to her physical stature weren't forthcoming. Instead, choreographers designed routines where they'd all dance on bent knees so that in a full wide frame, one couldn't tell that the hero would have been left leaning his head on her shoulder if only they'd been standing upright.

So she upped her game. She danced in ways no one could imagine a tall, awkward girl dances. She fought a lifelong battle against carbs; she made sure her face told a million stories so that's where the camera and the audience focused. And she discovered Manish Malhotra. Malhotra's classic chiffon silhouettes, flattering churidars and fluttering-in-the-breeze dupattas cemented her position as the diva the silver screen had been missing since Hema Malini.

Sometime in the late '90s the matrimonial ads changed.

Everyone wanted a five feet seven inches girl, minimum. Kareena, Sushmita, Aishwarya and Bipasha stormed into the industry. Then came Priyanka, Deepika, Sonam, Anoushka. Katrina, Jacqueline, Kangana. All these girls had style that celebrated their extra inches. The men still stood on stools in close-ups but in public, the girls stopped slouching. Sridevi, of course, had retired into marital life and her daughters were kept away from the glare of the press.

In 2010, Sridevi was one of the first star moms to post publicly on Instagram—from holidays abroad, shopping with her girls, at film previews and society weddings. Her daughters were ready for their very own debutante balls. In a photograph taken on a holiday abroad,[3] Janhvi looks coy and self-conscious like a young girl trying to channel the diva that her mother was to millions of Indians. She has the same vulnerable eyes, the lovely softness, but it's her sister that one cannot help but gawk at. A few years younger, this child-woman has legs that seem to stretch a mile and they are covered in a pair of knee-length boots. She's Khushi, Sridevi's younger daughter. And refusing to deny all five feet and ten inches of herself. In between the two young women stood Sridevi, shoulder blades razor straight, spine taut, chin high.

Film historian Praveish Vishwanath Aiyar, who also teaches cinema at Khalsa College in Mumbai, describes Sridevi's life as being in a state of perennial adjustment:

> She was constantly evolving: first into languages she did not speak, then into roles she was too young for and, later,

3. https://www.instagram.com/p/BPM3jSCBnfU/?hl=en&taken-by=sridevi.kapoor

> into a culture that was alien to her (Bollywood). It felt like she was always tentative, always unsure if she fit in, never revealing her true self. Acting therefore gave her the canvas for this—she could play act and live in the moment, be herself whenever she was in a frame. Even after she got married to Boney Kapoor, she was always trying to fit into his vision of the dream woman. In the constant struggle of within and without, the internal and the external, she often fell prey to other people's expectations vis a vis her insecurity. After all, Sivakasi to Mumbai is a long road to travel.'[4]

When Sridevi made a comeback with *English Vinglish,* although she chose the role of a mature woman with two children, she still had to look like Sridevi playing the part. She had to be the actress that her audience remembered, but better. So even though she was draped in elegant Sabyasachi sarees, her waist was the waist of youth, not of middle age. The fact that our attention never turned to the superficial things speaks of her true talent, even though she did seem to have set impossible standards for middle-aged beauty. Whether these standards were hers or someone else's is hard to tell, but she did pursue them with rigour. The same rigour that transformed her to her slimmer, chiselled *Chandni* avatar from her fuller, rough-at-the-edges *Himmatwala* one.

Let's face it. The Indian film industry is ageist when it comes to women and each one, whether Bollywood, Mollywood or Tollywood, has its own norms of beauty. When she entered Bollywood, her 'thunder thighs' were problematic and had to go. Her perky nose, which was good enough for

4. Interview, May 2018

the south, had to be chiselled into shape. It's just that in an attempt to make the chiselling perfect, after a point Sridevi no longer owned her features. There are moments in *English Vinglish* when you feel she is unable to smile or laugh with her own face. Botox had taken over a large part of it. If she wasn't a fine actress, that would have stood out like a sore thumb. Her hips (which were already contained by the time *Chandni* happened), were even slimmer now, and there was no trace of belly fat or wrinkles. For a woman of forty-nine, that is a tough act to pull off without interventions. In fact, barely a month before she passed away, there were reports going around of a lip job gone wrong.[5]

Because ageing gracefully is nearly impossible in showbiz. The benchmarks of beauty are impossibly high. Women in their forties and fifties are constantly under pressure to knock off years from their age, looking impossibly youthful and glamorous. The new stereotype for beauty is mother and daughter looking like sisters. It is well known that Sridevi and Janhvi were regulars at Dr Raj Kanodia's (Hollywood's celebrity plastic surgeon based in California), whose other eminent clients include Shah Rukh and Gauri Khan. Dr Kanodia's Instagram account is a testimony to their visits.[6]

Sridevi was not the first person to choose interventions to alter her appearance. But, unfortunately, she came under the scanner more frequently than the rest as her entire career was about alterations.

---

5. https://www.timesnownews.com/entertainment/fashion/article/the-curious-case-of-sridevis-lips-something-about-the-actress-looks-strikingly-different/192257

6. http://www.wionews.com/india-news/sridevi-the-tragedy-of-a-diva-34017

Sridevi's choice of 'look', her reported two-hour daily exercise regimen, her penchant for power yoga, dietary habits and cosmetic procedures were entirely her business. But her so called anorexia and falling victim to cosmetic procedures were analysed by many after her death, including by Shobhaa De in a Facebook post.

Her daughter Janhvi wasn't spared either.

In an interview to Upala KBR for *The Times of India,* Sridevi had once revealed that she wasn't keen that Janhvi act in films. 'I think people presume that because she is my daughter, she has to be an actor. I feel sad when people think I am an aggressive mother and I am pushing my daughter to join films or lose weight. I am extremely careful about my diet and workout and she follows me. In fact I play tennis with both my daughters twice a week. In fact recently one of the ladies in the health club told Jhanvi, "How sad to see you here, working so hard. Your mother must be making you do this, no?"'[7]

As women, we are constantly told to love ourselves for the way we are, to accept ourselves and not seek validation all the time. We are told we must age gracefully and not fall victim to the endless demands of beauty. We are told we are more than our body or our looks or our weight. We are encouraged to look at ourselves independent of the standards the world has set. Perhaps we didn't do this enough for Sridevi. Maybe we can at least do it for ourselves.

---

7. https://timesofindia.indiatimes.com/entertainment/hindi/bollywood/news/I-dont-want-Jahnavi-to-become-an-actor-Sridevi/articleshow/13133747.cms

10

The Yashraj Effect

Rang bhare baadal se
Tere nainon ke kaajal se
Maine is dil pe likh liya tera naam
Chandni… oh meri Chandni

(With the colours of the clouds
With the kohl of your eyes
I've written your name on my heart
Moonlight, you are my moonlight)

—Lyrics from *Chandni,* 1989

CHANDNI POLISHED SRIDEVI'S image—a Yash Raj patina that lasted all her life. She now had the finesse of a Yash Chopra heroine—grace, poise and confident vulnerability, which could be tailored into a brand statement. In turn, she gave us the iconic fitted white salwar kameez and *parandis* (hair extensions for braids) and showed us how to wear bangles and chiffon saris with panache.

Yash Chopra's career was on a downslide in the '80s, after having made a series of Indian cinema's most successful

Chandni, 1989

and celebrated films in the '70s, including the action thriller *Deewaar* (1975), which established Amitabh Bachchan as the leading actor of Bollywood, the romantic drama *Kabhi Kabhie* (1976) and *Trishul* (1978). By the late '70s, however, his films seemed to have lost their magic at the box office: *Doosra Aadmi* (1977), *Kaala Patthar* (1979), *Silsila* (1981), *Mashaal* (1984), *Faasle* (1985) and *Vijay* (1988) all bombed.

Then, in 1989, Chopra directed *Chandni,* the commercially and critically successful cult film, which became instrumental in ending the era of action films in Bollywood. 1988 and 1989 were the years in which romance and music returned to the movies, with *Maine Pyar Kiya* and *Qayamat Se Qayamat Tak,* launching Salman and Aamir Khan respectively. *Chandni* was as big a hit as the other two, even without a 'fresh young hero' as a hook.

Chandni was perhaps the first woman-centric film Yash Chopra ever made and its success proved that a woman could carry a romance on her shoulders just as well as a man. It appeared as though Mr Chopra had conceived the idea of the film entirely from the point of view of a woman, and then sought out an actress strong enough to play the part. His first choice was Rekha (she was the 'Chandni' in his last film, *Silsila*), but when she refused, he chose Sridevi.

'As an actress, she is one of the best we've ever had. She's far superior to all her contemporaries. She's more versatile than Rekha, who is the best among the rest. I had signed Sri for Chandni because she looked the central character, but I wasn't sure she would perform as well as Rekha. But after the first schedule, I was proud of my own choice. She's just terrific,' he said in the April 1989 issue of *Filmfare*.

In perhaps what would be one of the most intimate first-time encounters between a hero and a heroine, Rohit (Rishi Kapoor) accosts Chandni (Sridevi) during a blackout as she runs up to her room to fix a rip in her choli, which she discovers while dancing at a ladies' sangeet for her cousin who's getting married. (Unbeknownst to her, he has been a voyeur for the past few hours, watching her every move in '*Mere haathon mein*', capturing her through his camera.) Their eyes meet, their faces glow in the dark as Rohit flicks on his lighter. He says, 'There should be just enough light for you to look at me and for me to look at you.' In the next sentence, he declares his over-the-moon love for her, adding that Dilliwalas don't waste time on frivolities.

The narrative of *Chandni* was typical of a Yash Raj film love triangle. Two men are in love with the same woman; she loves one and respects the other. It explores the premise of unrequited love and its various permutations and combinations. Many scenes in the movie show photos of Sridevi on the wall, or montages of her as she is imagined by the men. The song '*Tu mujhe suna*' perhaps sums it up the best. The two (recent) friends, Lalit (Vinod Khanna) and Rohit, are sharing stories about the woman they fancy and although they are talking about the same woman, Chandni, their perceptions of her are so different. As the audience, you find this totally plausible, because only Sridevi can exist in that degree of polarity—of ebullience and containment, of playfulness and restraint, of charm and poise.

The movie created a whole new trend across India, 'the Chandni look'—the all-white salwar kameez ensemble, traditional, yet stylish churidar kurtas with ample, flowing dupattas in shocking pinks and yellows and, of course, lace and chiffon saris. Sridevi transforms in an instant from the poised to the playful, depending on how she moves in them. Bangle shops did booming business. Schoolgirls would click their wrists together to see who could impersonate her moves better. Parandis became cool. They were all trying to emulate her.

In her book, *Yash Chopra: Fifty Years of Indian Cinema*, Rachel Dwyer quotes Chopra from one of his interviews with her:

> I like working with Sridevi. She says, 'You do what you want.' We gave her a totally new look, jewellery, hairdo and costume. Bhanu Athaiya, who won an Oscar [for *Gandhi*], did all the dresses for the first schedule in Delhi but we had ego clashes and took Leena Daru. We had a lot of white, very simple clothes. We designed her saris and colours, middle-class salwars and churidars which changed when she was working but she could wear different clothes in the dream sequences, such as modern dresses.[1]

In the same book, Yash Chopra also speaks to Rachel about the big chance he took on Vinod Khanna, casting him as an out and out romantic hero.

> We began with a different treatment of the same film, more like an art film. We had a *mahurat* in November with Sridevi, Chintu [Rishi Kapoor] and Vinod Khanna. It was a romantic shot, with fantastic, beautiful people. In the first version, Sridevi marries Chintu, has a son. In the second half of January we went to Delhi. We started a two-day

1. https://scroll.in/reel/819198/chandni-turned-around-yash-chopras-fortunes-but-he-initially-called-it-a-suicide-attempt

> shoot. When mixing, I thought it was wrong and decided to change. The next morning I sat day and night changing the script to the interval. Sridevi said she had full faith in me. Chintu asked me to tell him the scenes. Vinod was an action-oriented hero, so there was to be a scene where he saves Sridevi from a fire. I cut it and rang up Sridevi and said I was going to repicturise it. The distributors were worried. How can you have Vinod Khanna and no action? One distributor even left the picture because I was taking Vinod Khanna in a non-action role. I wanted him because he was a mature person and would suit Sridevi. I gave them a discount so the terms were in my favour. I wanted a romantic film with beautiful music. I was sick of violence.

So inspired was Yash Chopra with Sridevi that he made another heroine-centric film with Sridevi in a double role in *Lamhe* (1991). The film was said to be 'ahead of its time' but Yash-ji knew that having a successful *Chandni* on his record was the right time to gamble with a *Lamhe*, an idea he had conceived a long time ago. When asked to choose a favourite film from his repertoire during a candid conversation with Karan Johar on television, Chopra pondered and said, 'Sometimes a film that you believe in doesn't get the love and affection from the audience that you hoped for. Then that becomes your favourite child. My two "neglected children", *Silsila* and *Lamhe*, remain my favourites. I'm especially proud of *Lamhe*. Maybe it was ahead of its time and didn't succeed at the box office. But it got me the biggest critical acclaim of my career.'[2]

Lamhe is as much the story of trans-generational love as unrequited love. Viren (Anil Kapoor) falls in love with older

2. https://www.youtube.com/watch?v=z1yh-Ipxu9U

Lamhe, 1991

woman Pallavi (Sridevi) who doesn't love him back. Pooja (Sridevi again) falls in love with the man who once loved her mother. Playing the mother and daughter, Sridevi was pitch-perfect. As Pallavi, she was dreamy and effervescent. As Pooja, she went from vulnerable and innocent to mature and sensitive with complete ease.

Sridevi was grateful to Chopra for this phase of her career. It lifted her in ways she hadn't experienced before. She said in an interview to *The Times of India* in 2012:

> I am grateful he gave me *Chandni* and *Lamhe.* These films are so special to me. If I have looked my best in these films, all the credit goes to Yash-ji. My saris and style in *Chandni* became a big craze. He was a trendsetter in every way. He was so organised that no discussions were needed on the sets. We would know which outfit goes with what scene. He was so involved yet would give us the freedom. He was not bookish. He would never say, *jo script mein hai wohi karna hai.* He was extremely friendly and childlike, always happy with no ego. I never felt he was an elderly filmmaker. His thoughts were fresh. He was extremely down-to-earth. He would never impose his thoughts on others, probably one of the only directors who listened to his assistant directors and actors. You don't see this quality in many.[3]

Yash Chopra wasn't done with Sridevi yet. He later offered her the role of Kiran in *Darr* (1993), but Sridevi said no and the role went to Juhi Chawla. Later Yash Chopra stated that Sridevi would not have suited the role as she would have

---

3. https://navbharattimes.indiatimes.com/movie-masti/interviews/i-am-grateful-yashji-gave-me-chandni-and-lamhe-sridevi/articleshow/16926170.cms

overpowered both the heroes in the movie. Juhi Chawla was accused of copying Sridevi in the song '*Tu mere samne*', where she dressed like Sri did in her Amrapali dress for *Chandni*'s tandav. Yash Chopra explained later that he had tried to give Juhi the *Chandni* look for the movie.

For Sridevi, *Lamhe* was her benchmark for what she expected from a Yash Raj film and she wouldn't settle for anything less.[4] It was perhaps for the same reason that she refused *Dil to Pagal Hai* (1997), which then resurrected Madhuri Dixit's career.

That's the exact thing Chandni would have done. She would have stood stoically and quietly for what she believed in, no matter what the world thought she ought to have done. Which is perhaps why every time you think of her, and imagine that life-sized *Chandni* poster on your wall, where she does a luxurious stretch (*angdayee*) in her white salwar kameez, you know it is as much about flexibility as about resoluteness.

---

4. https://sridevi.biz/roles-rejected-by-sridevi.html

11

Love, or Something Like That

Pehle pehle pyar ki pehli raat yaad rahegi
Phoolon ke is shehar ki mulakaat yaad rahegi
Kaash yahin saari umar yun hi jaaye beet jaaye mitwa
Aage aage chale hum, peechhe peechhe preet mitwa

(We will always remember the first night of our first love
We will remember this meeting of ours in this city of flowers
Wish we could spend our entire lives in this one moment
We walk hand in hand, love is always behind us.)

—Lyrics from *Chandni,* 1989

IN HER MOVIES, Sridevi experienced all kinds of love. Or the lack thereof.

In *Jaag Utha Insaan,* she played the Brahmin girl Sandhya, a temple dancer who is in love with Hari (Mithun), a flute player who is a Harijan (Dalit). The caste divide between them ensures that the match is doomed from the start.

In *Mr India,* she is in love with the idea of a man—larger than life, omnipresent, omnipotent, a saviour, a messiah, a destroyer of evil, and even an expert seducer. A man so amazing he had to be invisible.

In *ChaalBaaz,* love is about guzzling beer together (Manju) or having someone beat up goons to save her twin sister.

In *Chandni,* she is in love with Rohit (Rishi Kapoor), a man socially far from her equal and, later, almost ties the knot with a more mature, successful and compassionate Lalit (Vinod Khanna), who also happens to be her boss.

In *Judaai,* she is the woman who wants her man back, a man she has let go (actually sold) for a huge sum of money to a rich heiress who realises that there are after all a 'few good men' left.

In *Tohfa,* she sacrifices her love for her sister, who is in love with the same man.

In *Lamhe,* she is in love with someone who once loved her mother. It's a love that's unauthorised, out of the realm of 'normal', something she ought to get over. But she can't. And she doesn't.

In *Khuda Gawah,* her love affair with the man who risked everything in his life for her is marked by viraha, the pangs of parting.

In *Gumrah,* her suitor Rahul (Rahul Roy) betrays her, but it's her fan Jaggu (Sanjay Dutt) who becomes her friend in need and actually blossoms into her love.

In *English Vinglish,* the yearning is for respect rather than for love, a yearning to be heard, acknowledged; her desire is to feel that she matters.

But those were all in the movies. Real life was far more complicated for Sridevi. In real life, the men who actively pursued her were always already married to other women.

I remember one question frequently asked of Sridevi in magazine interviews in the '80s was: 'Do you date?'

Now whether this was asked in a derisive manner (would a woman who barely knows Hindi or English know what 'dating' means?), or whether it was asked out of genuine curiosity, or whether it was solely the film journalist's greed for salacious gossip is debatable, but let's give the premise the benefit of the doubt.

Dating, by definition, is the stage of a romantic relationship wherein two people meet socially with the aim of assessing each other's suitability as a prospective partner in an intimate relationship or marriage. It is a form of courtship consisting of social activities done by the couple, either by themselves or with others. While the term has several meanings, the most frequent usage refers to two people exploring whether they are romantically or sexually compatible by going on dates with the other.

Seems like an unattainable luxury for ordinary mortals in the 1970s and '80s. Ironically, even less so for a female superstar.

Is it really possible for a star to go for a walk or a swim, have a coffee or drink while she assesses the suitability of a prospective partner? When you have been on set practically every single day of your life, from the age of four, it must be hard to make real friends, forget a boyfriend. Even if you do, is there room to nurture the connection, away from the eyes of the whole world, which is actively sizing up the relationship and its future (or the lack of it)?

I met someone who went to the same tuition teacher as Sridevi on Periyar Road as a child. The kids always wanted to linger after class and play a little, but Sridevi, although gregarious and social, always had to be someplace else. In a few months, she didn't have time to even attend the tuitions, forget school. Of course her parents were around, and that was probably when she began to rely on the security blanket of the familiar. Any kind of newness, whether it was a relationship or a friend, was always outside her comfort zone. This also explains why, years after she started working in the Hindi film industry, she was still living in a hotel.

However, things changed after she achieved superstardom in Hindi films. Her parents, who had a home in Chennai, couldn't live with her long term. As she signed on more movies, her schedule got busier, and although her mother and sister managed her career and her administrative work, they couldn't always be with her.

Yes, suitors like Vijay Amritraj and Arvind Swamy had materialised in the south, but what about love? What of that irrational, elusive, feel good thing that you experience when you are in love? What of loving someone and being loved back? What of someone telling you, it's going to be okay, *main hoon na*? We all need that. Even Sridevi did.

There was youth and wilderness in this girl, who at long last wanted to live a little.

Yes, she was rich, she was successful, she was beautiful and many in the nation were vying for her, but she was lonely. She hardly ever had a chance to meet anyone outside the sets. That only left her co-stars and directors. She must have had the same question in her mind most women looking for love have. Where are the single men?

Often, they were not (single).

Like Mithun Chakraborty, whom Sridevi met on the sets of *Jaag Utha Insaan* (1984). There was a connection. There was chemistry. It was amply evident in the movie. Mithun had married Yogeeta Bali a few years ago (it was his second marriage), but he was enamoured of Sridevi nonetheless and the two spent a lot of time together and so the relationship blossomed. Sridevi, who was still trying to make a mark in Bollywood, found a friend and confidante in him, someone she could rely on, and soon they were in love. After her mother banned all films with Mithun, marriage seemed the only way out. However, Mithun had still not fulfilled his part of the bargain by making their relationship public and divorcing Yogeeta. The story after this has several versions that involve a secret marriage, a suicide attempt, a divorce/annulment, a series of 'no comments', a reconciliation and a happily ever after (not for Sridevi).

It was also the time that Boney Kapoor (who had recently married Mona Shourie) was keen to cast her for *Mr India* and did everything to make sure she said yes. (A few years later, in an interview to Rauf Ahmed, Boney said, 'My all-time favourite heroines have been Mumtaz, Tanuja, Hema and Rekha. Sridevi is a perfect blend of all four. There has never been a heroine like her. I wonder if there would be.'[1]

Interestingly, Mithun was also a good friend of Boney's. So now there was suddenly a triangle of sorts with two men (both married with kids) showering their attention upon Sridevi.

In later interviews, Boney would recall falling in love with Sri the very moment he met her to cast her for the role of Seema, the good-hearted, blabbering journalist in the 1987

1. *Filmfare*, April 1989

film. Boney produced the film with brother Anil Kapoor as the main lead.

Once the shooting for *Mr India* began, his love for her was expressed in the form of perks on the sets, like the best make-up room and the best costumes money could buy.[2] Sridevi, like any other young woman, started to feel special. After all, even a diva needs reassurance. And Mithun, like any man in love, was resentful. There was a hue and cry over these 'alleged favours'. Soon rumours of a rakhi ceremony followed (a traditional ceremony where sisters tie a symbolic thread on the wrists of brothers). At Mithun's request, Sridevi had drawn the line for Boney (or so the world thought) by making him her 'rakhi brother'.

But love knows no boundaries.

Eventually, Sridevi and Mithun went their separate ways.

The next few years were rough for Sridevi. She faced the death of her father, followed by the protracted illness of her mother. Her relationship with Boney had moved beyond friendship by now. He was her rock. It's possible she was looking for a father figure, like many women do. It's possible he started meaning more to her after her father died, that he filled a void. There are theories and theories. But love is flawed. Irrational. Inconvenient. Illogical.

It was the same story again though. Boney was a married man.

'Boney spelt security in her life. He was her constant

2. https://www.indiatoday.in/india-today-woman-summit/2013/video/sridevi-at-india-today-woman-summit-2013-417745-2013-04-19; www.indiatoday.in/movies/celebrities/story/sridevi-boney-kapoor-love-story-1180184-2018-03-01

support. And I think they learned to be inter-dependent,' says veteran film journalist Bhawana Somaaya. 'From Boney's side, it was an open declaration of love all the time. She was shy, never very articulate. But when he talked about her, she was always blushing. They had a very warm, loving equation.' Somaaya says Sridevi was not really seeking approval from Boney. 'It was a kind of a recheck or a reconfirmation. They both knew what had to be done.'[3]

At the India Today Woman Summit 2013, Boney recounted how their love blossomed. 'This is something which I enjoy talking about, and this is something which she doesn't want me to talk about,' he said. It seems Boney was smitten much earlier than he had let on. 'It happened the first time I saw her on screen; this was probably in the late '70s, when I saw one of her Tamil films. I said to myself that this is someone I would want to have in my film.'[4]

'I was determined to cast her in a film so I travelled all the way to her house in Chennai. She was shooting in Singapore at the time, and I could not meet her. But Sridevi refused to leave my thoughts. I watched her on screen in *Solva Sawan* next. Now, *Solva Sawan* is not a glamorous film, but somehow, she had some kind of impact on me which is hard to describe. She was on my mind all the time,' Boney said.

'I then decided to sign Sridevi for Shekhar Kapur's *Mr India*. I went up to her set, met her. When I met her, it was almost like a dream come true. You know, she is an introvert and doesn't communicate very easily with strangers, and I was a stranger at that point of time. The few words that she spoke

---

3. Interview in *The Week*, 11 March 2018
4. https://www.youtube.com/watch?v=noz1DKpfss8

in broken Hindi and broken English, they touched me and moved me, and I got more curious to know her,' he revealed.

Back then, it was Sridevi's mother who handled her professional meetings. When Boney flew to Chennai to meet her, she quoted a figure of ₹10 lakh. 'Sri was the highest paid heroine, and probably, this was her mother's way of negotiating. I heard her figure and I said "No, I'll pay ₹11 lakh." She thought I was a mad producer from Bombay who is offering more than what she'd asked for! Well, that's how I got close to her mother,' he said.

Every time Boney met Sridevi, he, in his own words, 'started getting more and more affected by her'. By now, he was head over heels in love with her. 'I was married then. In fact, I had confessed to my ex-wife that I was in love with her. I couldn't hold myself back,' he admitted.

And it was this love that made him follow Sridevi to Switzerland, where she was shooting for *Chandni*. Boney made an excuse for his presence, but his real mission was to see Sri.

Boney wanted to make her understand that he would always be there for her and, slowly, she began returning his love. 'She saw that this man was too persistent and perhaps realised that I was sincere and not looking for a ... fling. Somehow, things fell into place,' he said.

The couple finally tied the knot in 1996.

In the process people were hurt. Families. Children. Hearts were broken. His father, Surinder Kapoor, the renowned patriarch of the family, asked Boney to leave the family home. Sattee Shourie (Mona's mother and Boney's mother-in-law) slapped a legal notice on Sridevi, asking her to clarify her position regarding her marriage to Boney, which was null and void, since he was still legally married to Mona and had two children, Arjun and Anshula, with her. However, Mona Kapoor decided to be the bigger person and signed divorce papers since Sridevi was already with child.

Sridevi remained stoic and silent through it all. A few months later, their first daughter was born and Sridevi gave up her superstardom for the man she loved. Perhaps she set the stage, prompting a lot of other actresses to take the plunge as well. Madhuri Dixit, just before she married Dr Sriram Nene, said, 'Of course, an actress can put her career on hold for the man she loves. If Sridevi can do it, why can't I?'

Boney (she called him Papa) and Sridevi had two beautiful daughters, Janhvi (who recently made her debut in Karan Johar's *Dhadak* opposite Ishaan Khatter), and Khushi.

Sadly, Sridevi, who was excited about her daughter's first film, never got to see her on screen. Much like Mona Kapoor, who died two months before Arjun Kapoor's debut in *Ishaqzaade*.

12

Dhak Dhak: The Madhuri Effect

It was the April 1986 cover of *Filmfare* that announced Madhuri Dixit as 'The New Sensation'.

Not that it created a tremor in Sridevi's life. 'New sensations' like Kimi Katkar, Meenakshi Seshadri, Sonam, Padmini Kolhapure, Bhanupriya, et al were routinely making waves by then, but that hardly affected Sridevi because she was in a place all her own. After *Himmatwala,* she had been giving steady hits with *Jaani Dost, Maqsad, Mawaali* and *Justice Chaudhury,* among others, mostly remakes from the south with Jeetendra as the lead. Every third Sridevi film was a hit at the time. Of course there were debacles like *Aag aur Shola* and *Balidaan* and, later, *Sultanat* (whose claim to fame was the disastrous debut of Karan Kapoor) and *Bhagwaan Dada* (in which Sridevi does a dance number with Hrithik Roshan as a child artiste). However, she badly needed a solo blockbuster to up her game.

Nagina was released in November 1986 and declared the fluke hit of the decade. The March 1987 cover of *Filmfare* screamed 'DEVASTATING' and had Sridevi on the cover. She was now officially the highest paid star after Amitabh Bachchan.

Producer-director Manmohan Desai said in an interview to *Filmfare* in the same issue, 'With *Nagina,* Sridevi has shot out of the reach of most filmmakers. I can't afford to cast her in an Amitabh starrer any more. It's too risky a combination. Without bringing me extra *moolah,* it will increase the risk.'[1]

It was true. Sridevi had the power of the initial draw. Her name was enough to guarantee queues on opening day. Distributors were willing to buy a Sridevi movie as soon as it was announced. She could outlive even the most inept direction.

She followed it up with *Mr India* in 1987, a movie which proved her versatility as an out and out entertainer. Drama, comedy, song and dance, sex appeal—she had the whole package. Then with *Chandni* and *ChaalBaaz* (1989), she took her box office dependability to a whole new level where she outperformed all her competitors. Of course, she couldn't salvage everything that she appeared in—certainly not the grotesque *Himmat aur Mehanat* or *Watan ke Rakhwale, Sone pe Suhaaga* or *Pathar ke Insan.*

Meanwhile, Madhuri, who was just four years younger to Sridevi, was still on a slow start. After her disastrous debut in *Abodh* (1984), she had a string of flops and was playing second and third lead in movies like *Awara Baap, Swati, Manav Hatya* and *Mohre.* Then Subhash Ghai signed her on for *Uttar Dakshin* (1987) and *Ram Lakhan* (1989). At the time, her secretary Rikku Rakesh Nath handled Anil Kapoor's work, so he spoke to Boney Kapoor (Anil's brother) about her.

---

1. https://www.indiatoday.in/magazine/society-the-arts/films/story/19870630-sridevi-emerges-as-the-undisputed-empress-of-tinsel-town-the-highest-paid-indian-actress-799027-1987-06-30

'Boney took me to Subhash Ghai's office once, and all of us sat down together to decide how we would promote her. We decided to give an advertisement in *Screen* magazine, listing the names of producers like Shashi Kapoor, F.C. Mehra, Yash Chopra and Ashok Thakeria who were going to work with her. Most of them did not work with her, but we gave the ad anyway,' said Rikku in an interview to Rediff.com.[2] There was a time when Madhuri was willing to do even a small role in a Sridevi film if she was comfortable with the character.

One thing led to another and soon, Madhuri had signed *Tezaab* with N. Chandra, opposite Anil Kapoor. '*Ek do teen*' became a trailblazer and Anil Kapoor was now touting her as the next big thing. Although after *Tezaab*, she appeared for just fifteen minutes in *Ram Lakhan* and had a five-minute cameo in *Tridev* (both released in 1989).

Then the nineties came and things changed.

Movies became more teenybopper-ish—*Qayamat Se Qayamat Tak, Maine Pyar Kiya, Jo Jeeta Wohi Sikandar, Hum Aapke Hai Kaun*—heroes got younger, the Khans had made their entry. Madhuri was touted as this young beauty—a photographer's delight, with a near perfect face, amazing dancing skills and a thousand-watt smile. She was a trained Kathak dancer and spoke Hindi well, though she could not match Sridevi's versatility or comic timing.

Post 1989, Sridevi couldn't quite raise the bar. Her songs were not working the same magic as before, while Madhuri always had memorable song-and-dance sequences in each of her films. Even in her flop films, Madhuri's item numbers stood

---

2. http://www.rediff.com/movies/report/the-man-who-made-madhuri-dixit-a-star/20170515.htm

out: *Sailaab* (1990) with '*Humko aajkal hai intezar*', *Anjaam* (1994) with '*Chane ke khet mein*', *Yaraana* (1995) with '*Mera piya ghar aaya*', etc. Madhuri was a choreographer's delight and her songs outlived the movies she did.

By the early nineties, there were clearly two camps: the Sridevi camp and the Madhuri camp. Madhuri was becoming the toast of Bollywood's leading men, like Anil Kapoor, Sunny Deol, Jackie Shroff, Govinda, Aamir Khan, Shah Rukh Khan, Salman Khan, Sanjay Dutt, even an ageing Vinod Khanna; while Sridevi was getting restricted to Anil Kapoor and Rishi Kapoor, now that Jeetendra's career was over and she was no longer doing films with Mithun. Sridevi's Hindi (and her pronunciation) now began to matter because Madhuri had perfect diction.

Post *Chandni* and *ChaalBaaz* (1989), Sridevi had no solo hits or blockbusters in Bollywood for a while, although she was still shining in the south; while Madhuri was on a roll with *Dil, Saajan, Beta, Thanedaar* and *Khalnayak*. Then came *Hum Aapke Hain Kaun* (1994), which took Madhuri to superstardom, being India's biggest blockbuster at 300 crores.

Ironically, *Beta*, Madhuri's big blockbuster, was offered to Sridevi first and she turned it down. It ended up being a major hit in 1992 and consolidated Madhuri's position at a time when Sridevi's was slipping. *Beta* was written specifically for Sridevi; they'd even incorporated the song '*Dhak dhak karne laga*' for her. It was the Hindi version of the Telugu song '*Abbanee tiyyani*' from *Jagadeka Veerudu Athiloka Sundari*, Sridevi's blockbuster movie with Chiranjeevi, which was released in 1990. Even *Dil To Pagal Hai*, which Yash Chopra offered to Sridevi first in 1994, ended up resurrecting Madhuri's career in

1997 after the arrival of Karisma Kapoor and *Raja Hindustani* (1996).

I was never a big Madhuri fan, and have trouble recalling what she wore in her various item numbers, except in *Sailaab*. For '*Dhak dhak*' I remember it was something yellow, and I do remember her hair was always billowy. I also remember Sridevi was far more sensuous, with fewer chest thrusts in '*I love you*,' and somehow '*Dhak dhak*' seemed hugely inspired by it—from the lighting to the haystack.

With Sridevi, I remember every aspect of the ensemble in all her dances—wigs, headgear, feather dusters, the whole hog. Her songs came alive with the tiniest of details—sneezing to a feather duster here, an eye roll there, a cross eye here. I think visually Sridevi left a deeper mark. I am not talking beauty here. Madhuri was definitely a better dancer, but Sridevi had the real flair for performance.

Post *Chandni*, Sridevi had metamorphosed into a slim, sophisticated chiffon-clad siren. We saw shades of this even in *Khuda Gawah*, where she played mother and daughter, or *Gumrah*, where she plays an innocent girl arrested on drug charges, or even *Mr Bechara* (where nothing other than her made sense). In the '90s, Sridevi did fewer films, as her focus was on family. Despite that, she still reigned supreme, and commanded her price.

Post *Chandni* there were a series of flops—*Lamhe, Pathar Ke Insan, Farishtay, Naaka Bandi* and the biggest disasters of all—*Roop Ki Rani Choron Ka Raja* and *Heer Ranjha*.

She did have hits like *Khuda Gawah, Laadla, Gumrah* and *Judaai*, but they came nowhere near the magnitude of her '80s magic. It was time for Sridevi to move on. Perhaps marriage and motherhood gave her the legitimate exit option she was looking for and she took it gracefully post 1996.

Ironically, two years later, Madhuri left the industry to get married and move to Denver with her husband. It was as if she was following in Sridevi's footsteps.

13

Hiatus

In 1991, Sridevi was shooting for *Lamhe* close to Manchester in the UK when Yash Chopra received a call from Madras. It was Sridevi's mother, calling to say that her father had died. He didn't have the courage to break the news directly, so he told her that her father was critically ill and she must leave for Madras immediately. Yash-ji also let her know that if something went wrong, he would wait for her. Sridevi was back in sixteen days, once all the ceremonies around the death were concluded. The day she returned, they had to shoot a comic scene where she would have a mudpack on. Yash Chopra asked her if she was ready mentally and physically; she said she was there to do her job and that was to act.

Lamhe didn't do well at the domestic box office and both Yash Chopra and Sridevi were deeply saddened by it.

After *Lamhe,* she was offered *Darr* by Yash Chopra. But she turned it down saying, 'After *Chandni* and *Lamhe,* I feel *Darr* would have been an ordinary character for me. If I'm playing Shah Rukh Khan's role, then of course I would have loved to do it. The character Juhi played was new for her and so it was good for her. But for me, it was something I had done many times before.'

Darr made Juhi Chawla a superstar.

After *ChaalBaaz* and winning the Filmfare Award for Best Actress, she was the most exciting performer around. The audience had raised the bar but her directors were running out of ideas. The old formulas were done to death. She also had a string of flops following *Lamhe. Roop Ki Rani Choron Ka Raja* was a colossal disaster, as were *Pathar ke Insan, Naaka Bandi, Farishtay, Heer Ranjha, Lamhe, Gurudev* and *Chaand Kaa Tukdaa.*

Gurudev had some nice moments and Sridevi was in a double role again, but due to the huge delay in its release (owing to director Vinod Mehra's death), the film didn't really do well. She had rejected *Yugpurush* opposite Nana Patekar soon after signing it, stating she was not mentally prepared to play a prostitute. This annoyed him no end as he had already gone to town talking about 'working with Sridevi'. Apparently Anil Kapoor and Nana Patekar had a war of words on the set and Anil had walked out, so Boney urged her to walk out too.

Sri also spent an inordinate amount of time shooting for *Roop Ki Rani Choron Ka Raja,* Boney Kapoor's most ambitious project, in which she shimmied and contorted; her headgear and lenses were back and the sets and backdrops were even more opulent. 'It's not funny how I manage those crazy expressions on my face, with my eyes aching. I have to wear these lenses all day, and they hurt. But, sometimes, you end up giving more to a film than you normally do, because you like your role and the way it's shaping up.'[1]

---

1. https://www.filmfare.com/features/i-was-about-to-quit-late-sridevi-on-her-film-journey-26882-3.html

Roop Ki Rani Choron Ka Raja, 1993

The shooting of the film began with much fanfare in 1988 but constant delays meant the film hit theatres only in 1993. It's rumoured that the delay led to a heated debate between director Shekhar Kapur and producer Boney, which resulted in Shekhar being shown the door. That's when Satish Kaushik, his assistant, stepped in. The extravagant sets and song sequences coupled with Yash Chopra's request for Sridevi's shooting dates for *Chandni* (which Boney obliged) forced the film to miss its deadline multiple times. When the film was eventually released, it was a gamble that had gone horribly wrong; it was declared a disaster soon after release by trade pundits.

The initial budget earmarked for the film was ₹7 crore, which slowly climbed to ₹10 crore before the release. With such a huge budget, the stakes had become too high for the makers. Sridevi had invested her own money in the production of the film, apart from Anil Kapoor, who is said to have signed movies in bulk only to fund *Roop Ki Rani Choron Ka Raja*.

Meanwhile, Sridevi's sister, Srilatha, got married and moved back to Chennai. It was during this time that Boney Kapoor offered her emotional support. Boney's father asked her to move into their home in Versova as they felt being around a family in this trying time would be good for her. So she moved in. Very soon, she refused Pankaj Parashar's Hindi take on *Pretty Woman,* opposite Jackie Shroff. Boney wanted him to cast Anil Kapoor in the film, but Pankaj was reluctant. The film ultimately never got made.

Reacting to speculation that Boney was controlling her career, Sridevi said in a *Filmfare* interview in 1991: 'It's plain rubbish. Boney-ji is not controlling my career. Nobody can. Even when I was staying with Boney-ji's family, producers were free to meet me and I made my own decisions. I signed Mahesh Bhatt's *Gumrah* when I was there.'[2]

Her next hit was *Laadla* (1994) in which she spends most of her time slapping people or throwing things at them, exclaiming, 'Understand? You better understand!' at the drop

---

2. *Filmfare,* May 1991

of a hat. At the receiving end are random workers, Shakti Kapoor and Anil Kapoor. She is also slapped back occasionally (Anil Kapoor); and once she sets her car on fire. The film was a remake of a southern hit whose Tamil and Telugu versions were both offered to Sridevi but she had rejected them. When she was offered the Hindi version, she rejected it again and the role went to Divya Bharti. When Divya passed away, the role went back to Sridevi and turned out to be one of her three hits in the nineties.

Mr Bechara soon followed and Sridevi looked like the real bechara in it, trying to look earnest as a girl who has lost her memory while the people around her act like complete nincompoops. She has been handed over by her quack doctor-psychiatrist Anupam Kher to Anil Kapoor, who is missing a wife and trying to balance bottle-feeding a baby, running a printing press and ensuring that his pretend wife (Sridevi, of memory loss fame) does not give away the precious silver of his house to her pretend father, the crook (Shakti Kapoor, who for some reason, wears a lot of powder on his face and keeps parting his oil-drenched hair). Nagarjuna appears somewhere along the line and reminds Sridevi that he was engaged to her and things go downhill (literally and figuratively) from there.

In 1996, Sridevi was eagerly awaiting the release of *Army*. She believed the film would be a defining one in her career, as it was a revenge drama, *Sholay*-style. When asked why she was doing such a movie, she said, 'I think whatever our positive points are, once we get complimentary feedback, we overdo it so much that the audience gets fed up of it. For instance it happened with me. For every project they kept repeating the comedy element with me. Every time I had to roll my eyes and put on the same mischievous grin till it became monotonous. Which is why I make it a point to be different.'[3]

Army flopped miserably, and was a huge setback for her, despite the fact that the producers threw in a song with Shah Rukh at the last minute to cash in on his saleability. She believed she had paid the price for always having meatier roles than her heroes.

Sridevi had said before *Army*'s release to *Stardust*:

> I think I overdid the seductive numbers. I don't think any heroine, whether Madhuri or me or anyone else for that matter, can insist on an item number in every film. It's totally the producer's or director's choice. And if I have stopped doing such numbers, it's because I have graduated to doing different roles, like *Lamhe*, *Laadla* and *Khuda Gawah*, where the roles don't require me to do all this *jhatak mataks*. I think it's very important for an actress to grow, whatever the outcome, hit or flop. I hope I go down doing more projects like these, that are different.

She needed a new career strategy. She made choices which made people sit up and take notice. Choices she had never had to make so far. Taking a leaf out of Madhuri's book, she started signing movies with younger heroes. With teenage heartthrobs Salman Khan and Sanjay Dutt, who had together just delivered a hit in *Saajan* (opposite Madhuri Dixit). Then she agreed to do *Chandra Mukhi* (1993) opposite Salman, a fantasy film for which the script was written by Salman exclusively for Sridevi. Needless to say, the fantasy was short-lived and landed with a thud on its face. Interestingly, like her highs were compared

---

3. *Stardust*, July 1996

to Amitabh Bachchan's, so were her lows. Hers was a position similar to Big B's after *Agneepath.*

In *Gumrah,* she spends the first half of the movie in her bob and schoolgirl pigtails, gazing dolefully either at her piano or at Rahul Roy (who had debuted with *Aashiqui* in 1990) in a neon suit, and gives us some lovely watchable moments, especially in the jail scene. The fact that she had said yes to a role with Sanjay Dutt was a sign that Sridevi was doing everything possible and more to get her stardom back.

Sanjay had a history of being infatuated with Sridevi when she was in her prime, chasing her to every set and showing up at her make-up room, demanding to see her. She had actually asked for him to be dropped from *Khuda Gawah* (1992), and now this.[4] Sanjay was by then a very saleable star and so being in a movie with him would ensure a hit. Thankfully, it was and the audience loved her (and Sanju's pairing with her) in the movie.

But even in *Gumrah,* a movie she really thought would be a game changer, Sridevi looked like a student who had come fully prepared for her exams, while the others were just about winging it. Rahul Roy was trying to look sly, Reema Lagu had the look of someone who forgot to flush the toilet and Anupam Kher had spells of temporary insanity and rabidness. Only Sanjay Dutt was just being himself. The jail sequences were quite intense and so was the jailbreak, although Anupam Kher and Sunjay Dutt did actually go to a library to check out jailbreak ideas.

---

4. https://english.manoramaonline.com/entertainment/entertainment-news/2018/03/07/sridevi-refused-to-act-with-sanjay-dutt-after-this-dramatic-episode.html

I remember thinking: I think she should quit. What was she thinking doing the *awful Chandra Mukhi* or *Chaand Kaa Tukdaa*? I switched off at that point. When *Judaai* was released in 1997, I didn't even go and watch it; I was too scared. It was only a couple of years later that I watched it on television.

Rishi Kapoor, her co-star of five films, had said in an interview to *Stardust* in October 1993 that Sridevi was stagnating. 'She should stop making *those* faces,' were his words. Although taken aback by this statement, she handled it well. 'I don't know about this but I would like to tell you that I do what my directors tell me to. Tell me, how many variations can I possibly do with my face in the light and comedy scenes? I can only get variations in serious roles. Anyway since Chintu-ji has brought this to my notice I will keep this in mind and try not to repeat my expressions,' she said to *Stardust*.[5]

She took ageism by the horns when she was asked why she was signing films with younger stars like Salman and Akshay (*Meri Biwi ka Jawab Nahin*). 'Why didn't people ask me about this when I was doing films with N.T. Rama Rao who was from a totally different generation?' He'd been forty years her senior.

Apparently, she had also been chosen for *Baazigar* in 1993. She was supposed to play a dual role in the film and the script was written to suit her persona. However, the directors Abbas-Mustan then got uncomfortable with the idea of having Sridevi on board as they felt that the audience would never be able to sympathise with SRK's character if he killed her. The role was re-written and two newcomers, Shilpa Shetty and Kajol, were signed up.

---

5. http://sridevi.biz/stardust-october-1993.html

By 1996, she had married Boney Kapoor, making headlines as a home breaker.

I couldn't believe that after all these years, after such an amazing career, it was Sridevi's personal life that was the last thing etched in our memories before she quit. Thankfully, *Judaai* released the next year, and the magic was back not just on screen but at the box office. Sridevi didn't work for the next fifteen years, although there were a few false starts, like *Shakti* (which eventually went to Karisma) and her television show, *Malini Iyer*, which didn't exactly make TRP magic. It was the end of the superstar era, but the beginning of an era as a mother.

With her husband and daughters

14

Return of the Queen

AFTER FACING THE camera for three decades (1967-97), Sridevi finally took a break after the release of *Kaun Sachcha Kaun Jhootha* with Rishi Kapoor, when she was pregnant with her first daughter. She had tried hard to overcome the aftermath of her last batch of atrocious films, but even the success of *Judaai* (1997) didn't help. After that, she was in the new-motherhood zone, and didn't seem to care.

It's hard to believe that for a performer like Sridevi, who had been on camera since age four, her hiatus was perhaps the longest for any actress in Hindi cinema: almost fifteen years. She chose to immerse herself in PTA dates and open houses and, by her own admission, she was a hands-on mother. Her daughters were her priority.

In an interview with Subhash K. Jha after Feroz Khan passed away (2009), Sridevi had said: 'It's sad we've lost an actor and filmmaker who defined style and sophistication in our films. Where are the filmmakers like him?'[1]

She was perhaps referring to the dismal comeback offers

1. http://www.thaindian.com/newsportal/entertainment/sridevi-he-made-me-agree-to-do-janbaaz-by-speaking-tamil_100187239html.

she'd received. Like the one from Subhash Ghai, who wanted her to play a character role in *Yaadein* (2001) with Jackie Shroff but when Sridevi said no to this 'insignificant' role, it went to Rati Agnihotri. And thank god for that move because the only thing *Yaadein* is famous for was providing a playground for the Hrithik Roshan-Kareena Kapoor affair.[2]

B.R. Chopra wanted Sridevi to play the lead opposite Amitabh Bachchan in *Baghban* (2003) but she did not think of this as a suitable comeback vehicle. Hema Malini was signed instead, and it went on to become a super hit.

Then there was an almost comeback in her own production, *Shakti* (2002), a remake of Hollywood's *Not Without My Daughter*. But just before the shoot was to begin, Sridevi became pregnant with Khushi and she had to find a replacement. She offered Kajol the role but as she could not do it, Karisma Kapoor was signed. *Shakti* remains one of Karisma's strongest roles.

'Whatever I do now has to enthuse me and my audience. I can't just jump into it, for the sake of acting. It's very difficult for me to find the right vehicle to come back,' Sridevi had said then.[3]

But there was pressure. Things were not too hunky dory on the financial front. There were whispers of how she had tired of the spotlight and wanted nothing more than to be a wife and mother, but that she might have been compelled to get on to the battlefield to support her husband's many failed projects.

---

2. https://www.indiatoday.in/movies/gossip/story/hrithik-roshan-to-romance-kareena-kapoor-in-sanjay-guptas-next-rakesh-roshan-275317-2015-12-02

3. https://timesofindia.indiatimes.com/entertainment/hindi/bollywood/news/Feroz-persuaded-me-in-Tamil-Sridevi/articleshow/4471309.cms

After her parents' death, Sridevi was allegedly locked in a legal dispute with her sister and had to sign away a substantial portion of her properties in the south which were invested in her parents' names. Boney Kapoor had still not recovered from the huge losses of *Roop Ki Rani Choron Ka Raja* and had mortgaged his assets for another film, which never saw the light of day. Boney had then taken up a corporate job with Sahara's film and television network on a whopping salary.

Sridevi made her TV debut in the eminently forgettable *Malini Iyer* (2004), produced by husband Boney Kapoor, in which she played the earnest south Indian wife to a Punjabi husband (Mahesh Thakur). The series featured their many (clichéd) cultural misadventures when the couple moves to Punjab to stay with extended family.

Comebacks have always been hard for actresses. Madhuri Dixit's *Aaja Nachle* in 2007 was a disaster. Juhi Chawla, Karisma Kapoor, Kajol and Aishwarya Rai have all struggled with it. In an industry where men are ageless and women come with expiry dates, Sridevi couldn't be seen romancing the Khans who were technically older than her. What would the Anushkas and Deepikas do then?

Perhaps the only way Sridevi could make a comeback from such a pedestal was as a pure actor; so it became all the more important to choose the right moment and the right role, as the audience was willing to accept her more as a character than as a star. She needed to go back to her roots as a performer.

When *English Vinglish* released, it looked like a role tailor-made for Sridevi—a woman's struggle to fit in, her insecurity in not knowing a language that is considered cool. In a way, Sridevi changed the attitude of audiences towards Bollywood and what it stands for in the age of millennials. With two young daughters, she was familiar with the general condescension of today's youth to Hindi cinema, kids who were too 'netflixed' for their own good. *English Vinglish* was also a sly wink at her own struggles with languages (till the end, she spoke Hindi and English with a Tamil accent) and a movie that found resonance in a rising middle-class India, which still looked upon English as a marker of upward social mobility.

In her interview with me for this book, Anupama Chopra said:

> The thing about comeback films, say even for a Bachchan or Kajol, or Madhuri or several actors who did make a comeback is, they are so concerned about doing it well, about it being a commercial success, and also wanting to look a certain way, that they don't raise the bar. In that sense, *English Vinglish* for Sridevi was a very clever and perfect choice. She played her age, so she looked older, but still lovely. It was a smaller budget, contained film that really helped her leverage her many talents. Not for a minute in the movie did you feel that the actor has been away for fifteen years.

In *English Vinglish,* Sridevi plays a Maharashtrian woman, Shashi Godbole, who is challenged when it comes to speaking English. The movie had a sweet, subtle flavour to it that lingered, a true feel-good movie that the Indian audience could relate to. It's hard to believe Gauri Shinde when she says Sridevi was off her radar when she wrote *English Vinglish.*[4]

---

4. https://www.thehindu.com/features/cinema/an-experience-to-remember/article3790825.ece

Sridevi excelled in the role as only she could. The feeling of being lost in a crowd and being misunderstood was only too familiar. She took on the role and made it her own, and with her climactic speech in English at her niece's wedding, she emerged triumphant.

Fifteen years after her superstar days, she still had the chops to carry a movie on her shoulders. And we were reminded once again why the screen is where she always belonged and that when you let her fly, miracles could happen. She infused the part with just the right nuances of vulnerability, restraint and quiet strength, delivering a performance that was nothing short of perfect.

The movie was both a critical and commercial success and received wide acclaim overseas as well. *English Vinglish* was also India's official nomination for the Academy Awards for Best Foreign Film. Not a bad comeback for a forty-nine-year-old actress returning from the wilderness after a decade and a half.

She also made an attempt to regain her pan-Indian presence with the Tamil film *Puli* in 2015, a complete disaster for which she was paid a whopping sum. It was a choice one wishes she had never made. The film suffered huge losses and Sridevi never recovered from the fact that she had turned down *Baahubali* over money issues to face this!

Then *Mom* (2017) by Ravi Udyawar once again gave her the moments she was seeking—opposite Akshaye Khanna and Nawazuddin Siddiqui. Unlike *English Vinglish,* where she played a meek, nurturing mother, *Mom* delves into the moral dilemma of a mother out to avenge a horrific crime committed against her daughter. Sridevi infused Devki, her character, with a vulnerability and rage that made it so much more than a revenge saga.

Both *English Vinglish* and *Mom* were made by ad-filmmakers who grew up in awe of Brand Sridevi. Yet, they were able to leverage her talents quite cleverly. Both films were released in Telugu and Tamil as well.

'She's one of the few actors in the Hindi film industry ... who never looks jaded or old-fashioned. Although she's been working for five decades, her acting always looks today,' Akshaye Khanna had said in an interview to Anupama Chopra.[5]

In an interview to rediff.com after the success of *Mom*, Sridevi had said, 'I thought about my children and other family members, and how would they react to my character. Forget about me being Sridevi, no, I am a normal mother. I don't think or plan how it will become a commercial film. My approach to selecting a film is very simple—it should touch my heart.'[6]

It was also perhaps the first time that she had given so many interviews before and after a film's release and it was a sign that things had changed since she had gone on her break. 'Then, there wasn't much media. There was a mystery around the stars. It's different now, but that's fine. We have to live with that.'

5. https://www.youtube.com/watch?v=wwvnBdIyZ2I

6. http://www.rediff.com/movies/report/forget-me-being-sridevi-i-am-a-normal-mother/20170705.htm

15

Gone Too Soon

Yeh lamhe, yeh pal ham,
Barson yaad karenge,
Yeh mausam chale gaye toh,
Hum fariyaad karenge...

(We will remember these moments for years
Even when the seasons pass, we will request for them)

—Lyrics from *Lamhe,* 1991

ON 25 FEBRUARY 1983, *Himmatwala* was released and Sridevi stormed into the Hindi film industry, never to look back.

On 24 February 2018, on the twenty-second floor of Hotel Jumeirah Emirates Towers in Dubai, Sridevi breathed her last, leaving us all robbed of moonlight.

She was in the UAE to attend the wedding of Mohit Marwah, her nephew by marriage to Boney Kapoor. The initial reports stated cardiac arrest. Later, it was reported that she died of accidental drowning in the bathtub of her suite following a loss of consciousness.

In the post-mortem report, which went viral, the cause of death was stated as 'ACCIDENTAL DRAWNING [sic]'.

Fans raised a hue and cry.

One couldn't help recalling this excerpt that Sridevi had written for 'My Page' in *Stardust*, 1988:

> When I look back into the past, I can recollect one particular incident that shook me terribly. It happened while I was shooting for a Telugu film, along with ten to twelve other children. We were required to play in a lake, rather have a bath and then come out on the shore. We had given roughly four-five takes before the shot was finally okayed. I stepped out of the water, put on my clothes and sat a few metres away with my mother, awaiting further instructions. Suddenly, someone noticed that there was one more set of clothes lying on the grass, unworn... and as he desperately looked around he realized it meant only one thing—a child had drowned! Everyone was frightened. How would we inform his parents? The director sent a man to call the boy's mother immediately, while we waited anxiously.
>
> In some time, the mother of the child came all decked up in a beautiful saree, with flowers in her hair. She probably thought the director had liked her son's acting so much that he'd called her to congratulate her personally, maybe even to sign him for another film. The scene that followed was horrible. The director began by telling her how her son had met with an accident... And before he could finish, the lady screamed, 'Where is my son? I want to see my son.' The director remained silent. The lady became hysterical. She pulled her hair, flung the flowers away, tore her saree, banged her fists and rolled on the ground, crying, screaming and shouting at the same time. It was terrible. I don't think

> I'd ever forget that sight. Somehow it has helped me to grow up.[1]

Nothing made sense.

Fans were shocked at the circumstances surrounding her death and speculated that perhaps the family may have been aware of the 'real issues' and knew she was troubled. News channels cashed in on bathtub related TRPs while irate fans demanded an explanation, even if it was at the cost of her dignity. Some hurled accusations of a rushed, botched-up investigation, perhaps under political pressure. Some hinted at an underworld hand. Where is the detailed post-mortem report, why was a routine investigation not carried out, why was blood work not done, why were the lungs not checked for water, they asked.

New stories began to circulate to suggest she was not happy. Stories of anorexia, a punishing diet and possible cosmetic procedures were discussed mostly in negative terms. But what if she had aged just like other women? What stories would that have generated?

The case was closed, even as the questions were getting louder. A quick repatriation of the body was followed by a state funeral, with Sridevi wrapped in the tricolour. It didn't deflect the attention of the fans.

The who's who in their whites and sunnies were in full attendance at the funeral at Celebration Sports Complex, Lokhandwala, Mumbai, in the true tradition of paying respects to a film celebrity.

Families were united.

---

1. http://asridevi.blogspot.com/2010/10/sridevi-in-her-own-words.html

Conspiracy theories abounded.

The nation wanted to know.

They still don't.

Some spoke to TV channels. Others ranted on Twitter and Facebook. Parallels to the Whitney Houston case of 'death by accidental drowning' in the bathtub were drawn. Ram Gopal Varma wrote an open love letter to Sridevi, alleging that she was always unhappy beneath the façade. Delhi-based Sunil Singh, who is an ardent Sridevi fan and also a filmmaker, sought an independent probe into her death. Her net worth was quickly computed. Insurance policies were dug out—one allegedly taken out in Oman for ₹240 crore. The caveat was that the nominees could only claim the amount if she died in the UAE.

Singh initially filed a PIL seeking an investigation into Sridevi's death at the Delhi High Court on 9 March 2018,

Bidding adieu to a legend, 2018

arguing in his plea that Sridevi was five feet seven inches tall and the bathtub in which she'd drowned was only five feet long. He stated that her death was of national interest. After the High Court rejected his plea, he moved the Supreme Court, which also dismissed the petition.

Soon after Sridevi's death, the Indian media fought relentlessly over 'Whose Sridevi was she anyway?' Bollywood, Kollywood, Tollywood and Mollywood staked their claims, each one trying to obliterate the other. Members of the LGBT community paid tributes—remembering her beauty, celebrating her mischief, fun and sexiness.

Meanwhile the celebs tweeted, instagrammed, changed their DPs on social media, condoled the family and condoned the media for not letting her 'Rest in peace'.

An uncle, M. Venugopal Reddy, was interviewed by a Telugu TV channel, who said that he had nothing to hide and that he knew that financial troubles were weighing heavily on Sridevi's mind. He claimed that Boney Kapoor had incurred big losses due to which she had to sell some of her properties. He also mentioned that Sri had returned to acting primarily for financial reasons and that she had been deeply worried about her daughters' future financial security.

Srilatha put out a statement saying she would break her silence in forty-eight hours. Last heard, she was the recipient of Sridevi's Chennai properties and her husband issued a statement saying that they were on Boney Kapoor's side and that the uncle was a fraud.

For someone who strove so hard to lead a private life, it is rather painful to see that Sridevi's death was perhaps the most public *tamasha* of them all.

In her tribute to Sridevi in *Open* magazine, Rachel Dwyer delved into the psyche of the maligners. She wrote:

> Why do we listen to these stories when we don't know if they are true or not? Is it because it is hard for us to understand a rare creature like Sridevi, so much more beautiful, talented and famous than us? Perhaps we are jealous and think there has to be something odd about them and we can bring them down to our level? Perhaps we wish to divert attention from our own life stories, which may be dull but could look odd and incomprehensible under such scrutiny. More likely, we use stories about stars like Sridevi as ways of understanding ourselves. How much value do we put on looks? What should a woman do when she ages? How can someone so lovely have such problems? If we looked like that and had that lifestyle, our lives would be easy. Who deserves to be loved? Who should be happy?[2]

Most of us, including me, will never know who Sridevi really was. We will still believe we know her intimately, that we have that rare connection with her after spending so many hours watching her movies, feeling her joy, her sadness, her stillness and her movements.

For me, she will always be the broke Manju who walks into a bar alone and asks for beer but has too much self-respect to ask for credit.

Meanwhile, in the 'In Memoriam' section at the 2018 Oscars (Sunday, 4 March) was a picture of the late Indian

---

2. http://www.openthemagazine.com/article/sridevi-1963-2018/farewell-our-chandni-of-moonlit-romance

legend that was captioned 'Sridevi, actress'. Not 'Bollywood star'. Not 'Bollywood's first female superstar'. Not 'Female Amitabh'.

In just a few days, the hashtag #sonamkishaadi started trending more than #RIPSridevi.

Acknowledgements

THE HARDEST PART about writing the acknowledgements is knowing that no matter how hard you try, you are going to forget someone and hope that that someone will understand and forgive you.

The first thank you is to Sathya Saran, for popping the question, 'Do you want to write a Sridevi book?' at a residency in Hampi and then promptly connecting me to Debasri Rakshit, my editor at Westland, before I had a chance to think it through or get cold feet.

The second to Debasri, my calm, efficient, funny, multi-faceted, super sharp editor, who I also share a birthday with. Could the universe be more serendipitous? While she smiled at all the right places in the manuscript, she also shook me out of my fan girlhood at several points by saying, 'Now, do you really want to say *that*?'

To Vishwajyoti Ghosh, partner in design, who gave this book just that fun, zesty cover that embodies Sridevi.

To Adil Hussain, for your poignant foreword and for helping me understand Sridevi's craft a little better.

To Yashasvi Vacchhani, for all the help with the research and for your cheery spirit.

To Sumitra Chakraborty, the editor of *Stardust,* and Kamal Nath, who manages their library, for providing us smooth and uninterrupted access to their archives and granting permission to quote from them.

To Shaikh Ayaz, who told me, 'Talk to your mother', and who read the first chapter and said this was exactly the book on Sridevi he would want to read.

To Rachel Dwyer, for meeting me despite her busy schedule and sharing her thoughts and ideas and giving this project the nudge it needed. And for granting permission to quote from her articles and her book *Yash Chopra: Fifty Years of Indian Cinema.*

To Rauf Ahmed, for chai and conversations and all the stories you shared.

To Maithili Rao, for insights and inspiration through your book, *Smita Patil: A Brief Incandescence.*

To Jerry Pinto, for giving me the best piece of advice: 'Watch as many films as you can. How often do you get to do this?' For writing *Helen: The Life and Times of an H-Bomb.* For sharing words and wisdom.

To Khalid Mohamed, Baradwaj Rangan, Piyush Roy, Harish Iyer, Rauf Ahmed and Poonam Saxena, for granting permission to quote from your articles, anecdotes and interviews.

To Srividya Menon, for the many leads you provided. To Raedita Tandon, for connecting me to Srividya.

To Rachana Dubey, from *Bombay Times,* and Farhana Farook, from *Filmfare,* for being as generous as always with information and contacts.

To Zara Chowdhary, for your thoughts and words. Thank you for always being my bouncing board, seven seas notwithstanding.

To Arathi Menon, for being my 4 a.m. friend, and turning panic attacks into writing highs.

To Karishma Attari, for ideas and nods.

To the warm family at the National Film Archives in Pune: Veena, Niraj, Pooja, Arti and Prakash, for being so helpful during my research and photo gathering. For being as enthused as I was about this book.

To Re and Bravo (child and cat), for waiting patiently behind a closed door for me to surface every single day, while I was working on 'a very important project'.

To Amma and Maami, for being my repositories for all things south and for being able and willing decoders whenever a dialogue was too much for me to take.

To all my people who cheered me from the wings with 'Yays' and 'Yes you cans'.

And, lastly to Sridevi, wherever you are—for all the laughter and tears in the making of this book. You will always be my hero.